松涛館流空手道形教範全集
KATA GUIDE BOOK FOR ALL JAPAN KARATEDO SHOTOKAN

得意形 I　TOKUI KATA I
慈恩・観空大・抜塞大・五十四歩小・五十四歩大

慈恩
Jion

観空大
Kanku Dai

抜塞大
Bassai Dai

五十四歩小
Gojushiho Sho

五十四歩大
Gojushiho Dai

 一般財団法人全日本空手道松涛館

はじめに

Introduction

　松涛館流の空手道は船越義珍先生を始祖としますが、時代の流れとともに技術が継承される過程で形も微妙に変化しています。世界には松涛館流空手道の多くの愛好者がいるため、このことは一層顕著に現れています。このような現状を踏まえ、松涛館流空手道の技術を普及・継承する団体として松涛館流の形についての教範を刊行し、競技会や段審査における形の評価に資することにしました。

　すでに２０１６（平成２８）年に平安形及び鉄騎初段を基本形とする『松涛館流空手道形教範全集　基本形』を刊行しました。続編として『松涛館流空手道形教範全集　得意形』４巻を刊行する計画を立て、この度、その第１巻を刊行する運びとなりました。

　第１巻では、慈恩、観空大、抜塞大、五十四歩小、五十四歩大を取り上げています。これらの形は公式競技会等においては全日本空手道連盟第１指定形または得意形として演武されている形ですので、そのことを踏まえながら本法人の中央技術委員会で研究協議してまとめたものです。なお、慈恩、観空大は全日本空手道連盟の第１指定形を引用しております。

　加盟団体をはじめ関係者においてはそれぞれの団体で受け継がれた伝統は大切にしながら、競技会や審査会等においてはこの教範を活用していただき、本法人の得意形についての理解を深め、充実した指導や練習に活かしていただきたいと願っています。なお、この教範の写真と解説ですべてを伝えることには限界がありますので、本法人の講習会等でさら細部にわたって研究をしていただくようお願いします。

　本書の発行がさらなる空手道の発展につながることを祈念します。

２０１８（平成３０）年７月　　全日本空手道松涛館中央技術委員会

Shotokan-ryu Karatedo was founded by Funakoshi Gichin, but as the techniques have been passed down over time, the Katas have undergone subtle changes. This has become even more pronounced due to the fact that there are many enthusiasts of Shotokan-ryu Karatedo around the world. Our organization, which disseminates and passes down Shotokan-ryu Karatedo techniques, responded to this situation by publishing a manual of Shotokan-ryu Katas to assist in the evaluation of Katas at competitions and Dan examinations.

In 2016 we published "KATA GUIDE BOOK FOR ALL JAPAN KARATEDO SHOTOKAN - Kihon Kata", containing the Kihon Katas Heian Kata and Tekki Shodan, and now we are publishing a continuation in four volumes, "KATA GUIDE BOOK FOR ALL JAPAN KARATEDO SHOTOKAN - Tokui Kata".

Volume 1 of the book covers Jion, Kanku Dai, Bassai Dai, Gojushiho Sho, and Gojushiho Dai. Because Enbu of these Katas are carried out at venues such as official competitions, either as Japan Karatedo Federation-Daiichi Shiteigata or as Tokui Kata, the Central Technical Committee of our organization has taken this into consideration in its consultations and investigations for preparing of this volume. In the case of Jion and Kanku Dai, this volume quotes verbatim from the Japan Karatedo Federation's Daiichi Shiteigata.

It is our hope that member organizations and other parties involved will, without neglecting the traditions that have been passed down in their own organizations, make use of this manual in situations such as competitions and examinations, deepen their understanding of our organization's Tokui Kata, and use the manual to fill out their instruction and practice. However, because there is a limit to how completely the photos and commentary in this manual can convey the Katas, we request that you make use of the short courses, etc., that this organization offers in order to study the Katas in greater detail.

We pray that the publication of this manual will lead to an even greater flourishing of Karatedo.

July 2018　Central Technical Committee, All Japan Karatedo Shotokan

本書の活用にあたって
Using this manual

　一般財団法人全日本空手道松涛館は、公益財団法人全日本空手道連盟が制定している第1指定形（「慈恩」、「観空大」）及び第2指定形（「燕飛」、「観空小」）をそのまま形試合や段審査で使用することにしています。

　したがって、「慈恩」及び「観空大」の形は、公益財団法人全日本空手道連盟『空手道形教範　第1指定形』（2017．10.19　改訂版）から引用している関係上、技術用語も全日本空手道連盟空手道形教範の表記に合わせています。特に従来の「外受け」を「内受け」に、「内受け」を「外受け」に表記しておりますことを承知ください。

　また指定形については、よりわかりやすくするため、挙動の途中の写真を一部加えております。

At Kata Shiais and Dan examinations, All Japan Karatedo Shotokan uses, as-is, Daiichi Shiteigata (i.e., Jion and Kanku Dai) and Daini Shiteigata (i.e., Enpi and Kanku Sho) established by the Japan Karatedo Federation.
As a result, the Katas Jion and Kanku Dai in this manual are taken directly from Japan Karatedo Federation "KARATEDO KATA MODEL for TEACHING - Daiichi Shiteigata" (revised edition of October 19th, 2017), so the technical terms used for these Katas correspond to those used in the Federation's Karatedo Kata Model. In particular, please be aware that what is traditionally referred to as Sotouke is referred to here as Uchiuke, and vice versa.
As for Shitei Kata, we have added some photos of Kyodo in progress for your better understanding.

【引用文献・参考文献】
　公益財団法人全日本空手道連盟『空手道形教範　第1指定形』（2017.10 改訂版）

【参考文献】
　公益財団法人全日本空手道連盟『空手道教範』（2015.3 改訂版）
　公益財団法人全日本空手道連盟『空手道形教範　第2指定形』（2013.12 改訂版）
　一般財団法人全日本空手道松涛館『松涛館流空手道形教範全集　基本形』（2016.4）

もくじ
contents

慈恩　Jion ・・・・・・・・・・・・・・・ 7
　挙動一覧 ・・・・・・・・・・・・・・・・・・ 8
　各挙動解説 ・・・・・・・・・・・・・・・・ 14

観空大　Kanku Dai ・・・・・・・・・・ 35
　挙動一覧 ・・・・・・・・・・・・・・・・・・ 36
　各挙動解説 ・・・・・・・・・・・・・・・・ 44

抜塞大　Bassai Dai ・・・・・・・・・・ 73
　挙動一覧 ・・・・・・・・・・・・・・・・・・ 74
　各挙動解説 ・・・・・・・・・・・・・・・・ 80

五十四歩小　Gojushiho Sho ・・・・ 101
　挙動一覧 ・・・・・・・・・・・・・・・・・・ 102
　各挙動解説 ・・・・・・・・・・・・・・・・ 110

五十四歩大　Gojushiho Dai ・・・・ 137
　挙動一覧 ・・・・・・・・・・・・・・・・・・ 138
　各挙動解説 ・・・・・・・・・・・・・・・・ 144

（一財）全日本空手道松涛館のあゆみ

■ 2014年6月6日
「一般財団法人全日本空手道松涛館」を設立・登記

■ 2014年6月7日
公益財団法人全日本空手道連盟の評議員会において協力団体として承認

■ 2014年9月22日
（一財）全日本空手道松涛館設立記念祝賀会開催
（於　東京都・浅草ビューホテル）

■ 2015年7月12日
（一財）全日本空手道松涛館第1回全国空手道選手権大会開催
（於　東京都・日本武道館）

■ 2015年12月27日
全9地区協議会設立完了

■ 2016年4月
（一財）全日本空手道松涛館　『松涛館流空手道形教範全集　基本形』　発刊

■ 2018年7月
（一財）全日本空手道松涛館　『松涛館流空手道形教範全集　得意形Ⅰ』　発刊

慈恩
Jion
（47挙動）

おだやかな動きの中に激しい気魂のこもった形である。転身、転回、寄り足などを体得するのに適している形である。

練習に際しては特にむずかしい技はないが、平安、鉄騎の中にある種々の立ち方、技を正確に使って緩急のリズム、方向転換の際の手脚同時の基礎的動きが大切であり基本技を大変重んじた形である。

In this Kata, gentle movements are carried out with an intense spirit. This is a good Kata for mastering movements such as shifting, the pivot backstep, and the dragging step.

Practicing the Jion does not involve any particularly difficult Wazas, but it is a Kata that places great emphasis on Kihon Wazas, and in which fast and slow rhythms in the correct use of the various stances and Wazas in Heian and Tekki, and basic movements that involve moving hands and feet simultaneously when turning, are important.

＊従来の「外受け」を「内受け」に、「内受け」を「外受け」に統一した。
＊公益財団法人全日本空手道連盟『空手道形教範　第1指定形』（2017. 10. 19　改訂版）より引用。よりわかりやすくするため、挙動の途中の写真を一部加えております。（写真番号5、65）

慈恩　挙動一覧

慈恩　各挙動解説

直立 ①

礼 ②

直立 ③

用意 ④

【手の動作】
両手は開いて大腿部両側につけて伸ばす。

【足の動作】
結び立ち。（左右とも正面に対して約30度）

※礼をする。

【手の動作】
手はそのまま。

【足の動作】
立ち方はそのまま。

【手の動作】
右拳を左掌で包み、下顎前に拳2つくらい離して構える。両肘の間隔は肩幅程度。

【足の動作】
結び立ちから閉足立ちになる。

【Hands】
Open both hands and stretch the arms down to the sides of the thighs.

【Feet】
Musubidachi (left and right feet are angled approximately 30 degrees from front).

※ Bow (Rei).

【Hands】
Same as in ①.

【Feet】
Same as in ①.

【Hands】
Wrapping right fist with left palm, hold hands in front of lower part of jaw about two fists distance away. Space between both elbows is about shoulder width.

【Feet】
Move from Musubidachi to Heisokudachi.

【手の動作】
両拳を胸前で交差させる。

【足の動作】
左足を北へ引く。

【手の動作】
右中段外受け、左下段受け。

【足の動作】
右前屈立ち。

【手の動作】
両拳を胸前で交差して（右手、手前）ゆっくりしぼる。

【足の動作】
左足を1歩南東へすり出す。

【手の動作】
両拳中段掻き分け受け（甲斜め上向き）。

【足の動作】
左前屈立ち。

【Hands】
Cross the arms in front of the chest.

【Feet】
Pull left leg back toward North.

【Hands】
Right-Chudan-Sotouke. Left-Gedanuke.

【Feet】
Right-Zenkutsudachi.

【Hands】
Tensing slowly, cross both fists in front of the chest (Right hand nearest chest).

【Feet】
Make one step out with the left leg toward southeast.

【Hands】
Chudan-Kakiwakeuke with both arms, back of the hand facing diagonally upwards.

【Feet】
Left-Zenkutsudachi.

挙動3	挙動4	挙動5	挙動6
 ❾	 ❿	 ⓫	 ⓬

【手の動作】
手はそのまま。

【足の動作】
南東へ右中段前蹴り。左脚立ち。

【留意点】
前蹴りをするとき、手を引かない。

【手の動作】
右中段順突き。左拳は左腰に引く。

【足の動作】
右足を南東へおろし、右前屈立ち。

【留意点】
挙動3～4は連続する。

【手の動作】
左中段逆突き。右拳は右腰に引く。

【足の動作】
立ち方はそのまま。

【手の動作】
右中段順突き。左拳は左腰に引く。

【足の動作】
立ち方はそのまま。

【留意点】
挙動5～6は連続する。

【Hands】
same as in ❽.

【feet】
Right-Chudan-Maegeri to southeast.

【Note】
Don't pull the hands back when executing Maegeri.

【Hands】
Right-Chudan-Juntsuki. Pull back left fist to the left hip.

【Feet】
Right foot is placed down toward Southeast, into Right-Zenkutsudachi.

【Note】 Motion 3 - 4 must be done continuously.

【Hands】
Left-Chudan-Gyakutsuki. Pull back right fist to the right hip.

【Feet】
Same as in ❿.

【Hands】
Execute Right-Chudan-Juntsuki continuously. Pullback left fist to the left hip.

【Feet】
Same as in ❿.

【Note】
Motion 5 - 6 must be done continuously.

挙動1～6の解釈

途中	挙動7	挙動8	挙動9

⑬	⑭	⑮	⑯

【手の動作】
両拳を胸前で交差して（右手、手前）ゆっくりしぼる。

【足の動作】
左脚を軸に右足を南西へゆっくりすり出す。

【手の動作】
両拳中段搔き分け受け（甲斜め上向き）。

【足の動作】
右前屈立ち。

【手の動作】
手はそのまま。

【足の動作】
南西へ左中段前蹴り。右脚立ち。

【留意点】
前蹴りをするとき、手を引かない。

【手の動作】
左中段順突き。右拳は右腰に引く。

【足の動作】
左足を南西へおろし、左前屈立ち。

【留意点】
挙動8～9は連続する。

[Hands]
Tensing slowly, cross both fists in front of the chest (Right hand nearest chest).

[Feet]
Keeping body weight on the left foot, slowly move right foot toward southwest.

[Hands]
Chudan-Kakiwakeuke with both arms, back of the hand facing diagonally upwards.

[Feet]
Right-Zenkutsudachi.

[Hands]
Same as in ⑭.

[Feet] Left-Chudan-Maegeri to southwest.

[Note]
Don't pull the hands back when executing Maegeri.

[Hands]
Left-Chudan-Juntsuki. Pull back right fist to the right hip.

[Feet]
Left foot is placed down toward Southwest, into Left-Zenkutsudachi.

[Note]
Motion 8 - 9 must be done continuously.

◀道着を掴んでいる相手の両腕に両拳を入れ、中段搔き分け受けをする。さらに中段蹴りをして、順突き、逆突き、順突きと中段を連続攻撃する。

Against an opponent grabbing your dogi, insert both hands between the opponent's arms and execute Chudan-Kakiwakeuke. Then, attack with Chudangeri, Junzuki, Gyakuzuki and Junzuki to the Mid-section in combination.

挙動10	挙動11	途中	挙動12

⑰	⑱	⑲	⑳

【手の動作】
右中段逆突き。左拳は左腰に引く。

【足の動作】
立ち方はそのまま。

【手の動作】
左中段順突き。右拳は右腰に引く。

【足の動作】
立ち方はそのまま。

【留意点】
挙動10〜11は連続する。

【手の動作】
右掌をいったん額前に上げ、左拳は左腰に引く。

【足の動作】
左足を南へ移動させる。

【留意点】
途中の姿勢で止まらない。

【手の動作】
左上段揚受け。右拳は右腰に引く。

【足の動作】
左前屈立ち（半身）。

【Hands】
Right-Chudan-Gyakutsuki. Pull back left fist to the left hip.

【Feet】
Same as in ⑯.

【Hands】
Execute left-Chudan-Juntsuki continuously. Pull back right fist to the right hip.

【Feet】
Same as in ⑯.

【Note】
Motion 10 – 11 must be done continuously.

【Hands】
Immediately raise right open hand to in front of forehead while pulling back left fist to the left hip.

【Feet】
Move left foot toward south.

【Note】
Do not stop at this point.

【Hands】
Left-Jodan-Ageuke. Pull back right fist to the right hip.

【Feet】
Left-Zenkutsudachi (Hips in Hanmi position).

挙動 13	途中	挙動 14	挙動 15
㉑	㉒	㉓	㉔

【手の動作】
右中段逆突き。左拳は左腰に引く。

【足の動作】
立ち方はそのまま。

【手の動作】
左掌をいったん額前に上げ、右拳は右腰に引く。

【足の動作】
右足を南へ進める。

【手の動作】
右上段揚受け。左拳は左腰に引く。

【足の動作】
右前屈立ち（半身）。

【手の動作】
左中段逆突き。右拳は右腰に引く。

【足の動作】
立ち方はそのまま。

【Hands】
Right-Chudan-Gyakutsuki. Pull back left fist to the left hip.

【Feet】
Same as in ⑳.

【Hands】
Immediately raise left open hand to in front of forehead while pulling back right fist to the right hip.

【Feet】
Advance right foot toward south.

【Hands】
Right-Jodan-Ageuke. Pull back left fist to the left hip.

【Feet】
Right-Zenkutsudachi (Hips in Hanmi position).

【Hands】
Left-Chudan-Gyakutsuki. Pull back right fist to the right hip.

【Feet】
Same as in ㉓.

途中	挙動16	挙動17	途中
 ㉕	 ㉖	 ㉗	㉘

後ろ

【手の動作】
右掌をいったん額前に上げ、左拳は左腰に引く。

【足の動作】
左足を南へ進める。

【手の動作】
左上段揚受け。右拳は右腰に引く。

【足の動作】
左前屈立ち（半身）。

【手の動作】
右中段順突き。左拳は左腰に引く。

【足の動作】
右足を南へ進め、右前屈立ち。

【留意点】
気合い。

【手の動作】
両拳開掌。両腕をいったん胸前で交差する。

【足の動作】
右脚を軸に体を左に回転させ、左足を西へ移す。

【Hands】
Immediately raise right open hand to in front of forehead while pulling back left fist to the left hip.

【Feet】
Advance left foot toward south.

【Hands】
Left-Jodan-Ageuke. Pull back right fist to the right hip.

【Feet】
Left-Zenkutsudachi (Hips in Hanmi position).

【Hands】
Right-Chudan-Juntsuki. Pull back left fist to the left hip.

【Feet】
Step south with the right foot, into Right-Zenkutsudachi.

【Note】
Kiai.

【Hands】
Both hands are open and flat, and should be immediately crossed in front of the chest.

【Feet】
Pivoting right foot turn the body to left and bring left foot to west.

| 挙動18 | 挙動19 | 途中 | 挙動20 |

【手の動作】
両腕を互いに引っ張り合うようにして、右拳右側面上段受け。左拳左側面下段受け。

【足の動作】
右後屈立ち。

【手の動作】
右鉤突き。左拳は左腰に引く。

【足の動作】
左足を西へ進め、右足を引きつけ（寄り足）、騎馬立ち。

【手の動作】
両拳開掌。両腕をいったん胸前で交差する。

【足の動作】
東を向く。

【手の動作】
両腕を互いに引っ張り合うようにして、左拳左側面上段受け。右拳右側面下段受け。

【足の動作】
左後屈立ち。

【Hands】
Moving at the same time, right hand executes Sokumen-Jodanuke, while left hand executes Sokumen-Gedanuke.

【Feet】
Right-Kokutsudachi.

【Hands】
Right-Kagitsuki. Pull back left fist to the left hip.

【Feet】
Advance with left foot toward west, dragging right foot (Yoriashi) into Kibadachi.

【Hands】
Both hands are open and flat, and should be immediately crossed in front of the chest.

【Feet】
Face east.

【Hands】
Moving at the same time, left hand executes Sokumen-Jodan-Uke, while right hand executes Sokumen-Gedan-Uke.

【Feet】
Left-Kokutsudachi.

挙動18～19の解釈

◀相手の中段蹴りを左側面下段受けする。さらに寄り足で鉤突きをして中段を攻撃する。

Defending the left side, block opponent's Chudangeri with Gedan-Uke. Then, moving in with Yoriashi, attack Chudan with Kagitsuki.

挙動21	途中	挙動22	途中

後ろ / 後ろ / 後ろ

【手の動作】
左鉤突き。右拳右腰に引く。

【足の動作】
右足を東へ進め、左足を引きつけ（寄り足）、騎馬立ち。

【手の動作】
左拳は右肩上、右拳は斜め下に出す。

【足の動作】
左足を北へ進める。

【手の動作】
左下段払い。右拳は右腰に引く。

【足の動作】
左前屈立ち（半身）。

【手の動作】
右掌底を側面から横に回す。

【足の動作】
右足を北へ1歩進める。

【Hands】
Left-Kagitsuki. Pull back right fist to the right hip.

【Feet】
Advance with right foot toward east, dragging left foot (Yoriashi) into Kibadachi.

【Hands】
Prepare for the next move by moving left fist to right shoulder and crossing the right arm diagonally down in front of the left hip.

【Feet】
Step left foot toward north.

【Hands】
Left-Gedanbarai. Pull back right fist to the right hip.

【Feet】
Left-Zenkutsudachi (Hips in Hanmi position).

【Hands】
Turn the right palm sideways.

【Feet】
Step once toward north with right foot.

挙動 23	挙動 24	挙動 25	途中
㊲	㊳	㊴	㊵
後ろ	後ろ	後ろ	

【手の動作】
右掌底右側面中段横受け。左拳は左腰に引く。

【足の動作】
騎馬立ち。

【手の動作】
左掌底左側面中段横受け。右拳は右腰に引く。

【足の動作】
左足を北へ1歩進め、騎馬立ち。

【手の動作】
右掌底右側面中段横受け。左拳は左腰に引く。

【足の動作】
右足を北へ1歩進め、騎馬立ち。

【手の動作】
両拳開掌。両腕をいったん胸前で交差する。

【足の動作】
右脚を軸に体を左に回転させ左足を東へ移す。

[Hands]
Right-Shotei-Right-Side-Sokumen-Chudan-Yokouke. Pull back left fist to the left hip.

[Feet]
Kibadachi.

[Hands]
Left-Shotei-Left-Side-Sokumen-Chudan-Yokouke. Pull back right fist to the right hip.

[Feet]
Take one step toward north with left foot, into Kibadachi.

[Hands]
Right-Shotei-Right-Side-Sokumen-Chudan-Yokouke. Pull back left fist to the left hip.

[Feet]
Take one step toward north with right foot, into Kibadachi.

[Hands]
Both hands are open and flat, and should be immediately crossed in front of the chest.

[Feet]
Pivoting on right foot turn the body to the left and bring left foot toward east.

◀相手の中段順突きを左掌底で中段横受け。

Block opponent's Chudan-Junzuki with a sideways block with left palm.

挙動26	途中	挙動27	途中

㊶	㊷	㊸	㊹

【手の動作】
両拳を互いに引っ張り合うようにして、右拳右側面上段受け。左拳左側面下段受け。

【足の動作】
右後屈立ち。

【手の動作】
右拳はそのまま、左拳を右脇腹に持っていく。

【足の動作】
立ち方はそのまま。

【手の動作】
左拳左側面上段諸手受け、右拳は左肘内側に添える（甲下向き）。左肘は左肩の高さ。

【足の動作】
左足に右足を引きつけ、閉足立ち。

【手の動作】
両拳開掌。両腕をいったん胸前で交差する。

【足の動作】
右足を西へ進める。

【Hands】
Moving at the same time, right hand executes Sokumen-Jodan-Uke, while left hand executes Sokumen-Gedan-Uke.

【Feet】
Right-Kokutsudachi.

【Hands】
Keeping right arm in the same position, bring left fist to the right flank.

【Feet】
Same as in ㊶.

【Hands】
The Left arm blocks left-side Jodan-Morote-Uke, with the right fist aligned with the inside of the left elbow. The left elbow should be shoulderheight.

【Feet】
Pull right foot to left foot, into Heisokudachi.

【Hands】
Both hands are open and flat, and should be immediately crossed in front of the chest.

【Feet】
Step right foot toward west.

挙動28	途中	挙動29	途中

 ㊺  ㊻  ㊼  ㊽

【手の動作】
両腕を互いに引っ張り合うようにして、左拳左側面上段受け。右拳右側面下段受け。

【足の動作】
左後屈立ち。

【手の動作】
左拳はそのまま、右拳を左脇腹に持っていく。

【足の動作】
立ち方はそのまま。

【手の動作】
右拳右側面上段諸手受け、左拳は右肘内側に添える（甲下向き）。右肘は右肩の高さ。

【足の動作】
右足に左足を引きつけ、閉足立ち。

【手の動作】
右拳を顔前から左肩前に動かし、体の正面で両手を交差。

【足の動作】
立ち方はそのまま。

【留意点】
顔を南へ向けながら、ゆっくり両手を動かす。途中の姿勢で止まらない。

【Hands】
Moving at the same time, left hand executes Sokumen-Jodanuke, while right hand executes Sokumen-Gedanuke.

【Feet】
Left-Kokutsudachi.

【Hands】
Keeping left arm in the same position, bring right fist to the left flank.

【Feet】
Same as in ㊺.

【Hands】
The right arm blocks rightside Jodan-Morote-Uke, with the left fist aligned with the inside of the right elbow. The right elbow should be shoulder-height.

【Feet】
Pull left foot to right foot, into Heisokudachi.

【Hands】
Bring right fist to the left shoulder, moving across the front of the face, and cross both arms in front of the body.

【Feet】
Same as in ㊼.

【Note】
While moving to face south, move the hands slowly. Do not stop at this point.

| 挙動30 | 途中 | 挙動31 | 挙動32 |

【手の動作】
両拳両側に掻き分け。

【足の動作】
立ち方はそのまま。

【手の動作】
両拳（両甲下向き）を両脇腹に引く。

【足の動作】
右足を南へ大きく踏み込み、左足を引きつける。

【留意点】
途中の姿勢で止まらない。

【手の動作】
両拳で下段交差受け（右手上、両甲外側）。

【足の動作】
右足前交差立ち。

【手の動作】
両拳を両側の下段に掻き分ける。

【足の動作】
左足を北へ引き、右前屈立ち。

【Hands】
Spread both fists down to the both sides of the body and hold them there.

【Feet】
Same as in ㊼.

【Hands】
Bring both hands to the sides of the hips, with the backs of both hands facing downward.

【Feet】
Take a large step toward south with right foot, then pull in left foot.

【Note】
Do not stop at this point.

【Hands】
With the right fist on top, Gedan-Kousauke.

【Feet】
With the right foot in front, Kousadachi.

【Hands】
Pull both fists apart, executing Gedan-Kakiwakeuke to both sides of the body.

【Feet】
Pull left foot back toward north, into Right-Zenkutsudachi.

途中

【手の動作】
両拳を胸前で交差（右手前）する。

【足の動作】
左足を南へ進める。

【Hands】
Cross both hands in front of the chest, right hand in front.

【Feet】
Step toward south with left foot.

挙動 33

【手の動作】
両拳中段掻き分け受け（両甲前向き）。

【足の動作】
左前屈立ち。

【Hands】
With both hands, Chudan-Kakiwakeuke (backs of the hands facing forward).

【Feet】
Left Zenkutsudachi.

挙動 34

【手の動作】
両拳で上段交差受け（右手外）。

【足の動作】
右足を南へ進め、右前屈立ち。

【Hands】
Jodan-Kosauke with both fists (right fist in front).

【Feet】
Step towards South with Right foot, into Right Zenkutsudachi.

挙動 35

【手の動作】
右裏拳上段打ち。左拳はそのまま。

【足の動作】
立ち方はそのまま。

【Hands】
Execute Right-Uraken-Jyodanuchi. Left fist stays where it is.

【Feet】
Same as in (55).

挙動 36	挙動 37	途中	挙動 38
 ⑤⑦	 ⑤⑧	 ⑤⑨	⑥⓪
		 後ろ	 後ろ

【手の動作】
左拳中段突受け、右背腕上段流し受け（甲裏向き）。

【足の動作】
立ち方はそのまま。

【手の動作】
右裏拳上段打ち。同時に左腕は水月の前に添える。

【足の動作】
立ち方はそのまま。

【留意点】
挙動35～37は連続する。

【手の動作】
右拳を前に出し、左拳を右脇腹にもっていく。

【足の動作】
右脚を軸に体を左に回転させて左足を西へ移動させる。

【留意点】
途中の姿勢で止まらない。

【手の動作】
左中段外受け。右拳は右腰に引く。

【足の動作】
左前屈立ち（半身）。

【Hands】
Execute Left-Fist-Chudan-Tsukiuke with Right Haiwan-Jyodan-Nagashiuke.

【Feet】
Same as in ㊹.

【Hands】
While executing Right-Uraken-Jyodanuchi, hold left arm in front of solar plexus.

【Feet】
Same as in ㊹.

【Note】
Motion 35-37 must be done continuously.

【Hands】
Extend right fist in front, bring left fist to the right flank.

【Feet】
Pivoting on the right foot turn the body to the left and bring left foot toward west.

【Note】
Do not stop at this point.

【Hands】
Left-Chudan-Sotouke. Pull back right fist to the right hip.

【Feet】
Left-Zenkutsudachi (Hips in Hanmi position).

◀右上段突きを右前屈立ちで上段交差受け。ただちに右裏拳上段打ち。
すかさず相手が左上段突きをするのを、右背腕上段流し受け。ただちに右裏拳打ちをする。同時に左腕は左手甲を右肘に接し、水月前に添える。

挙動34～37の解釈

| 挙動 39 | 途中 | 挙動 40 | 挙動 41 |

【手の動作】
右中段順突き。左拳は左腰に引く。

【足の動作】
右足を西へ1歩進め、右前屈立ち。

【手の動作】
左拳を前に出し、右拳を左脇腹にもっていく。

【足の動作】
左脚を軸に体を右に回転させて右足を東へ移動させる。

【留意点】
途中の姿勢で止まらない。

【手の動作】
右中段外受け。左拳は左腰に引く。

【足の動作】
右前屈立ち（半身）。

【手の動作】
左中段順突き。右拳は右腰に引く。

【足の動作】
左足を東へ1歩進め、左前屈立ち。

【Hands】
Right-Chudan-Juntsuki. Pull back left fist to the left hip.

【Feet】
Take one step west with right foot, into Right-Zenkutsudachi.

【Hands】
Extend left fist in front, bring right fist to the left flank.

【Feet】
Turn the body to the right and step right foot forward to east.

【Note】
Do not stop at this point.

【Hands】
Right-Chudan-Sotouke. Pull back right fist to the right hip.

【Feet】
Right-Zenkutsudachi (Hips in Hanmi position).

【Hands】
Left-Chudan-Juntsuki. Pull back right fist to the right hip.

【Feet】
Take one step east with left foot, into Left-Zenkutsudachi.

Block opponent's Right-Jyodantsuki with Jyodan-Kosauke in Right-Zenkutsudachi. Right-Uraken-Jyodanuchi immediately after Kosauke.
When opponent attacks with Left-Jyodantsuki, immediately block with Right Haiwan-Jyodan-Nagashiuke. Counter immediately with Right-Jyodan-Uraken-Uchi, while placing left arm in front of . Back of left hand touches right elbow.

| 途中 | 挙動42 | 途中 | 挙動43 |

⑥⑤　　　　　　⑥⑥　　　　　　⑥⑦　　　　　　⑥⑧

後ろ　　　　　　後ろ　　　　　　後ろ　　　　　　後ろ

【手の動作】
左拳は右肩上、右拳は左斜め下に出す。

【足の動作】
左足を北へ移す。

【手の動作】
左下段払い。右拳は右腰に引く。

【足の動作】
左前屈立ち（半身）。

【手の動作】
右拳は頭上高く振り上げる。左拳そのまま。

【足の動作】
右膝を高くあげて北へ踏み込む。

【手の動作】
右拳右側面中段打落とし。左拳を左腰に引く。

【足の動作】
騎馬立ち。

【Hands】
Prepare for the next move by moving left fist to right shoulder and crossing the right arm diagonally down in front of the left hip.

【Feet】
Bring left foot toward north.

【Hands】
Left-Gedanbarai. Right fist pulls back to the right hip.

【Feet】
Left-Zenkutsudachi (Hips in Hanmi position).

【Hands】
Lift right fist above head. Keep left hand in the same position as ⑥⑥.

【Feet】
Lift right knee high, then stamp down toward north

【Hands】
Right side Chudan-Uchiotoshi with right fist. Pull left fist back to left hip.

【Feet】
Kibadachi.

| 途中 | 挙動44 | 途中 | 挙動45 |

【手の動作】
左拳は頭上高く振り上げる。

【足の動作】
左膝を高くあげて北へ踏み込む。

【手の動作】
左拳左側面中段打落とし。右拳を右腰に引く。

【足の動作】
騎馬立ち。

【手の動作】
右拳は頭上高く振り上げる。

【足の動作】
右膝を高くあげて北へ踏み込む。

【手の動作】
右拳右側面中段打落とし。左拳を左腰に引く。

【足の動作】
騎馬立ち。

【Hands】
Lift left fist above head.

【Feet】
Lift left knee high, then stamp down toward north.

【Hands】
Left side Chudan-Uchiotoshi with left fist. Pull right fist back to right hip.

【Feet】
Kibadachi.

【Hands】
Lift right fist above head.

【Feet】
Lift right knee high, then stamp down toward north.

【Hands】
Right side Chudan-Uchiotoshi with right fist. Pull left fist back to left hip.

【Feet】
Kibadachi.

◀相手の中段順突きを右中段打落しで叩き落とす。

Hip down opponent's Right-Chudantsuki with Right-Chudan-Uchiotoshi.

挙動44の解釈

途中	挙動46	途中	挙動47

73	74	75	76

【手の動作】
体を回転させながら右掌は左肩前。左拳（甲上向き）は右脇。

【足の動作】
右脚を軸に体を左に回転させ左足を引きつけながら東へ移動させる（寄り足ぎみ）。

【留意点】
ゆっくり。

【手の動作】
両腕を交差し、互いに引きしぼる。右拳右乳前（甲上向き）。左拳左側面中段突き（甲上向き）。

【足の動作】
騎馬立ち。

【手の動作】
顔を西へむけると同時に左掌は右肩前、右拳（甲上向き）は左脇。

【足の動作】
立ち方はそのまま。

【手の動作】
両腕を交差し、互いに引きしぼる。左拳は左乳前（甲上向き）、右拳は右側面中段突き（甲上向き）。

【足の動作】
右足を西へ移し、左足を引きつけ（寄り足）て、騎馬立ち。

【留意点】
気合い。

【Hands】
While turning the body, ready the right palm in front of left shoulder. Position left fist at right flank, back of the hand facing upward.

【Feet】
Pivoting right foot turn the body to the left, then, slide left foot to east (drag) (Similar to Yoriashi).

【Note】
Do slowly.

【Hands】
Cross both arms and squeeze them inside. Right fist comes in front of the right breast (back of hand faces upward) and execute Left-side Sokumen-Chudantsuki with left fist.

【Feet】
Kibadachi.

【Hands】
While facing west, left palm comes in front of the shoulder, pull back right fist (back of hand faces upward) to the side body.

【Feet】
Same as in 74.

【Hands】
Cross both arms and squeeze them inside. Right fist comes in front of the left breast (back of hand faces upward) and right side Chudantsuki (back of hand faces upward) with right fist.

【Feet】
Move right foot toward west, and, pull left foot drag(Yoriashi).

【Note】
Kiai.

挙動46の解釈

◀相手の右中段順突きを右掌でつかみ、引き寄せながら、左拳左側面中段突き。

While taking hold of opponent's Right-Chudan-Juntsuki and drawing with right palm, execute Left-Sokumen-Chudantsuki with left fist.

止め	直立	礼	直立

❼❼	❼❽	❼❾	❽⓿

【手の動作】
右拳を左掌で包み下顎前に構え、用意の姿勢に戻る。

【足の動作】
右足を左足に引きつけ、閉足立ち。

【手の動作】
両手は開いて大腿部両側につけて伸ばす。

【足の動作】
結び立ち。

※礼をする。

【手の動作】
手はそのまま。

【足の動作】
立ち方はそのまま。

【Hands】
Wrapping right fist with left hand, position both hands in front of jaw before returning to 'Yoi' position.

【Feet】
Pull right foot up to left foot, into Heisokudachi.

【Hands】
Open both hands and stretch them along both thighs respectively.

【Feet】
Musubidachi.

※ Bow (Rei).

【Hands】
Same as in ❼❽.

【Feet】
Same as in ❼❽.

観空大
Kanku Dai
(65 挙動)

この形は四方、八方に敵を仮想して各方向からの様々な攻撃を捌き、受けて反撃するもので非常に変化の富んだ形である。技の緩急、力の強弱、体の伸縮はもちろん、転回、飛び上り、伏せなどがあり大変難しい形である。

This Kata is full of variety; it hypothesizes enemies all around and involves shifting, blocking, and counterattacking in response to a variety of attacks coming from different directions. In addition to the presence of fast and slow Wazas, the use of more or less force, and stretching and contracting of the body, the Kanku Dai features movements such as pivoting, jumping, and lying down, making for an extremely difficult Kata.

*従来の「外受け」を「内受け」に、「内受け」を「外受け」に統一した。
*公益財団法人全日本空手道連盟『空手道形教範　第1指定形』(2017. 10. 19　改訂版) より引用。よりわかりやすくするため、挙動の途中の写真を一部加えております。(写真番号5、16、19、23、25、27、37、46、50、52、54、56、58、60、71、73、75、78、84、90、105)

観空大　挙動一覧

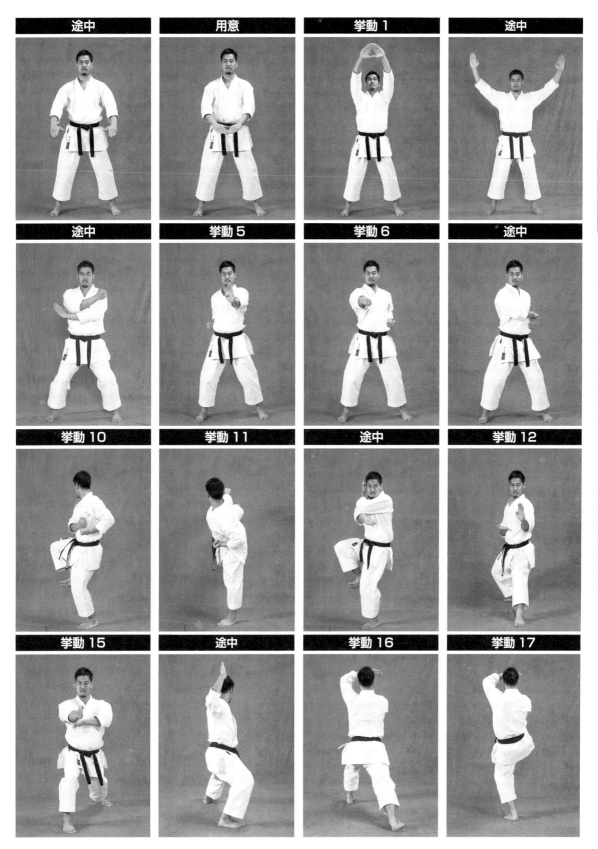

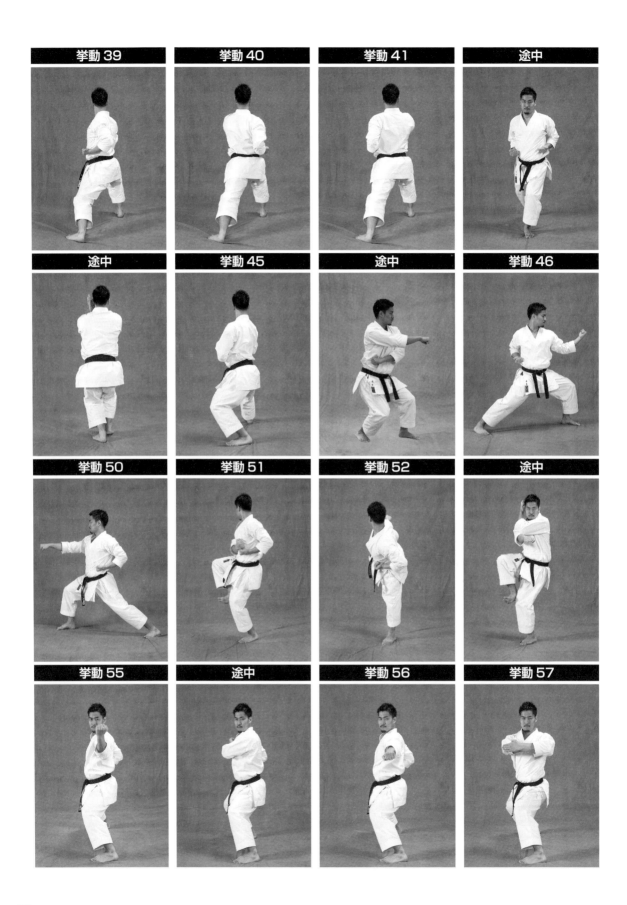

観空大　各拳動解説

 ① 直立

 ② 礼

 ③ 直立

 ④ 途中

【手の動作】
両手は開いて大腿部両側につけて伸ばす。

【足の動作】
結び立ち。（左右とも正面に対して約30度）

※礼をする。

【手の動作】
手はそのまま。

【足の動作】
立ち方はそのまま。

【手の動作】
両拳を大腿部前にもっていく。

【足の動作】
左足、右足の順に開いて八字立ち。

【Hands】
Open both hands and stretch the arms down to the sides of the thighs.

【Feet】
Musubidachi (left and right feet are angled approximately 30 degrees from front).

※ Bow (Rei).

【Hands】
Same as in ❶.

【Feet】
Same as in ❶.

【Hands】
Bring both fists to in front of the thighs.

【Feet】
From Musubidachi, move the left foot, then right foot, out into Hachijidachi.

【手の動作】
両拳を開く。

【足の動作】
立ち方はそのまま。

【手の動作】
静かにゆっくり両掌を右を上に親指同士、中指同士を重ねる。

【足の動作】
立ち方はそのまま。

【手の動作】
両掌を重ねたまま額斜め上に（途中の姿勢で止まらない）。

【足の動作】
立ち方はそのまま。

【留意点】
ゆっくり。指の間から空を観る気持ちで（目の高さより手の動きに合わせる）。

【手の動作】
両掌を左右に速く開く。

【足の動作】
立ち方はそのまま。

【留意点】
開くとき、止めない。

【Hands】
Open both hands.

【Feet】
Same as in ④.

【Hands】
Place both palms in front of the body with right palm on top. The thumbs are placed together, so are the middle fingers.

【Feet】
Same as in ④.

【Hands】
While placing right palm on left palm, lift them diagonally above forehead (Do not stop at this point).

【Feet】
Same as in ④.

【Note】
Do slowly.
As if looking up to the sky between fingers (follow your hands upward when they reach eye level).

【Hands】
Spread both palms swiftly to each side.

【Feet】
Same as in ④.

【Note】
Do not interrupt the motion after opening the arms.

45

途中	挙動2	挙動3	挙動4

⑨	⑩	⑪	⑫

【手の動作】
両掌は止めずにゆっくりと両肘を軽く伸ばし静かに弧を描き、下腹部前へもっていく。

【足の動作】
立ち方はそのまま。

【留意点】
途中の姿勢で止まらない。

【手の動作】
左掌を縦に（甲斜め左下向き）右掌は左掌の上に斜めに軽く重ねる（右甲下向き）。

【足の動作】
立ち方はそのまま。

【手の動作】
左背腕左側面上段受け（左甲北向き）。右掌胸前に構える（右甲下向き）。

【足の動作】
八字立ちより左足を東へすり出して、右後屈立ち。

【留意点】
後屈立ちの重心の割合は後足7、前足3のバランス。

【手の動作】
右背腕右側面上段受け（右甲北向き）。左掌胸前に構える（左甲下向き）。

【足の動作】
方向を西へ変え、左後屈立ち。

【留意点】
挙動3〜4はサッと早く続ける（腕の動きより後屈立ちに注意）。

【Hands】
Bring both palms down slowly without stopping to the front of lower abdomen. Stretch both elbows lightly and describe an arc slowly.

【Feet】
Same as in ④.

【Note】
Do not stop at this point.

【Hands】
Left palm is vertical, (with back of hand facing diagonally downward to the left). Right hand is placed lightly on left palm (back of hand facing downward to the right).

【Feet】
Same as in ④.

【Hands】
Left-Haiwan-Left side Jyodan-Uke (back of left hand faces north). Hold open right hand in front of chest (back of right hand faces downward).

【Feet】
From Hachijidachi, slide left foot toward east into Right-Kokutsudachi.

【Note】
For Kokutsudachi, the body weight is distributed 70% on the back leg, 30% on the front leg.

【Hands】
Right-Haiwan-Right side Jodan-Uke (back of right hand faces north). Hold left palm in front of chest (back of left hand faces downward).

【Feet】
Turn and face west, into Left-Kokutsudachi.

【Note】
Motion 3 - 4 must be done quickly. Pay attention more to Kokutsudachi than arm movement.

◀右上段順突きを左背腕左側面上段受けで受ける。

Block opponent's Right-Jodan-Junzuki using Left-Haiwan-Left side Jyodan-Uke.

挙動3の解釈

| 途中 | 挙動5 | 挙動6 | 途中 |

⓭　　　　　　　⓮　　　　　　　⓯　　　　　　　⓰

【手の動作】
右拳を左肩前にもっていく。左掌は右肘下からゆっくり大きく弧を描き前に出す。

【足の動作】
左後屈立ちから右脚を軸にして八字立ちになる。

【手の動作】
左中段縦手刀受け。右拳右腰に引く。

【足の動作】
膝を軽く伸ばし、八字立ち。

【留意点】
ゆっくり。

【手の動作】
右中段突き。左拳左腰に引く。

【足の動作】
立ち方はそのまま。

【手の動作】
右拳を左脇腹にもっていく。左拳はそのまま。

【足の動作】
立ち方はそのまま。

【Hands】
Position right fist at left shoulder. Left palm draws out in a large arc, starting from under the right arm.

【Feet】
Keeping the weight on the right leg pull the left leg in to Hachijidachi.

【Hands】
Left-Chudan-Tate-Shutouke. Pull right fist to the right hip.

【Feet】
Knees are slightly bent, stay in Hachijidachi.

【Note】
Do slowly.

【Hands】
Right-Chudantsuki. Pull back left fist to the left hip.

【Feet】
Same as in ⓮.

【Hands】
Bring right fist to left side of the body. Keep left fist in the same position as ⓯.

【Feet】
Same as in ⓮.

挙動7	挙動8	途中	挙動9

⑰	⑱	⑲	⑳

【手の動作】
右中段外受け。左拳はそのまま。

【足の動作】
八字立ちより足の位置そのままで腰を左転し、左膝屈。

【留意点】
膝屈を正確に。両足が床面に密着すること（特に後足刀部）。

【手の動作】
左中段突き。右拳右腰に引く。

【足の動作】
八字立ち。

【手の動作】
左拳を右脇腹にもっていく。右拳はそのまま。

【足の動作】
立ち方はそのまま。

【手の動作】
左中段外受け。右拳はそのまま。

【足の動作】
八字立ちより足の位置そのままで腰を右転し、右膝屈。

【留意点】
膝屈を正確に。両足が床面に密着すること（特に後足刀部）。

【Hands】
Right-Chudan-Sotouke. Keep left fist same as in ⑯.

【Feet】
Twist hips to the left without changing location of feet. Bend left knee(Left-Hizakutsu).

【Note】
Bend the knee correctly. Both feet must stick to the floor firmly (especially the edge of back foot).

【Hands】
Left-Chudantsuki. Pull back right fist to the right hip.

【Feet】
Hachijidachi.

【Hands】
Bring left fist to right side of the body. Keep right fist in the same position as ⑱.

【Feet】
Same as in ⑱.

【Hands】
Left-Chudan-Sotouke. Keep right fist same as in ⑱.

【Feet】
Twist hips to the right without changing location of feet. Bend right knee(Right-Hizakutsu).

【Note】
Bend the knee correctly. Both feet must stick to the floor firmly (especially the edge of back foot).

| 挙動10 | 挙動11 | 途中 | 挙動12 |

【手の動作】
右拳（甲前向き）を左拳の上（甲下向き）に重ね、両拳左腰構え。

【足の動作】
右膝屈より左足を半歩引き寄せ、左脚を軸として腰を右転。右足裏を左膝横に添え、左脚立ち。

【留意点】
両拳をしっかりと左腰に引く。

【手の動作】
右裏拳上段横回し打ち。左拳そのまま。

【足の動作】
北へ右横蹴上げ。

【留意点】
横蹴上げの場合、上体が力み過ぎて引手が横蹴上げと同時に離れないこと。

【備考】
蹴上げ（目標中段）。

【手の動作】
左手刀は右肩上、右手刀（甲上向き）は左斜め下に出す。

【足の動作】
左脚を軸に、体を南へ向けながら蹴り足を引き、北へおろす。

【手の動作】
左手刀中段受け。右手刀胸前。

【足の動作】
右後屈立ち。

[Hands]
Hold both fists on the left hip, with right fist (back of fist facing outside) on top of the left fist (back of fist facing downward).

[Feet]
Pull left foot half step forward from Right-Hizakutsu and stand on the left foot, then, pivoting on left foot, turn hips to the right. Place right foot sole lightly on the left knee.

[Note]
Firmly pull both fists back to the left hip.

[Hands]
Jodan-Yokomawashiuchi with Right-Uraken. Left fist same as in ㉑.

[Feet]
Right-Yokokeage toward north.

[Note]
For Yokokeage, avoid tensing the upper body too much, and that the pulled hand doesn't come away from the body when kicking. Keage is Chudan.

[Hands]
Position Left-Shuto above the right shoulder. With the back of the right hand facing up, extend Right-Shuto diagonally downward to the left.

[Feet]
While turning south and keeping weight on left leg, pull in kicking leg and then put down toward north.

[Hands]
Left-Shuto-Chudan-Uke. Hold Right- Shuto in front of the chest.

[Feet]
Right-Kokutsudachi.

【手の動作】
右手刀は左肩上、左手刀（甲上向き）は右斜め下に出す。

【足の動作】
右足を南へ1歩進める。

【手の動作】
右手刀中段受け。左手刀胸前。

【足の動作】
左後屈立ち。

【手の動作】
左手刀は右肩上、右手刀（甲上向き）は左斜め下に出す。

【足の動作】
左足を南へ1歩進める。

【手の動作】
左手刀中段受け。右手刀胸前。

【足の動作】
右後屈立ち。

【Hands】
Position Right-Shuto above the left shoulder. With the back of the left hand facing up, extend Left-Shuto diagonally downward to the right.

【Feet】
Take right foot one step toward south.

【Hands】
Right-Shuto-Chudan-Uke. Hold Left-Shuto in front of the chest.

【Feet】
Left-Kokutsudachi.

【Hands】
Position Left-Shuto above the right shoulder. With the back of the right hand facing up, extend Right-Shuto diagonally downward to the left.

【Feet】
Take left foot one step toward south.

【Hands】
Left-Shuto-Chudan-Uke. Hold Right-Shuto in front of the chest.

【Feet】
Right-Kokutsudachi.

挙動 15	途中	挙動 16	挙動 17

㉙	㉚	㉛	㉜

	後ろ	後ろ	後ろ

【手の動作】
右中段四本貫手（甲右向き）。左掌中段押え受け（右肘下、甲上向き）。
【足の動作】
右足を南へ1歩進め、右前屈立ち。
【留意点】
①気合い、②前屈立ちを正確に。足刀及び足裏を床面に密着させる。
【備考】
足刀及び足裏の床面に対する密着はすべてに言える。

【手の動作】
右手刀を右肩上、左手刀を下段にもっていく。
【足の動作】
右脚を軸に腰を左転し北へ向く。
【留意点】
途中の姿勢で止まらない。

【手の動作】
右手刀上段横回し打ち。左掌額前上段受け。
【足の動作】
左前屈立ち（逆半身）。

【手の動作】
手はそのまま。
【足の動作】
右前蹴り。左脚立ち。

【Hands】
Right-Chudan-Shihon-Nukite (back of hand facing east). Left-Palm- Chudan-Osaeuke (underneath right elbow, back of hand facing upward).
【Feet】
Take right foot one step toward south, Right-Zenkutsudachi.
【Note】
① Kiai ② Zenkutsudachi must be performed accurately. Both Sokuto (edge of foot) and Ashiura (sole of foot) should keep firm contact with floor. This applies throughout the Kata.

【Hands】
Position Right-Shuto above right shoulder, and Left-Shuto to Gedan.
【Feet】
Pivoting on right foot, turn hips to the left, facing north.
【Note】
Do not stop at this point.

【Hands】
Jyodan-Yokomawashiuchi with Right-Shuto. Left-palm-Jyodan-Uke in front of forehead.
【Feet】
Left-Zenkutsudachi (hips in reverse Hanmi).

【Hands】
Same as in ㉛.
【Feet】
Right-Maegeri. Stand on the left foot.

挙動 16 の解釈

◀相手の右中段蹴りを左手刀で下段受けして、右掌を右肩上から半円を描き相手の首を打つ。

Block the opponent's Right-Chudangeri with Left-Shuto-Gedan-Uke, and strike the opponent's neck with the right hand drawing a semi-circular motion to from above the right shoulder.

途中	挙動18	挙動19	挙動20

㉝	㉞	㉟	㊱

【手の動作】
左掌は右肩上、右掌（甲下向き）は左斜め下に出す。

【足の動作】
左脚を軸に、体を南へ向けながら蹴り足を引き、北へおろす。

【留意点】
途中の姿勢で止まらない。

【手の動作】
右拳右側面上段受け。左拳左側面下段受け。

【足の動作】
右後屈立ち。

【留意点】
両掌を握りながら互いに引き絞るように受ける。

【手の動作】
右手刀下段打込み（甲下向き）。左掌上段流し受け（甲横向き）。

【足の動作】
右脚を軸に、左前屈立ち。

【手の動作】
左拳下段に伸ばす。右拳右腰に引く。

【足の動作】
左足を右足にすこし引き寄せ、左足前レの字立ち。

【留意点】
ゆっくり。

【Hands】
Position left palm above the right shoulder. With the back of the right hand facing up, extend right palm diagonally downward to the left.

【Feet】
While turning south and keeping weight on left leg, pull in kicking leg and then put down toward north.

【Note】
Do not stop at this point.

【Hands】
Right fist Right side Jyodan-Uke. Left fist Left side Gedan-Uke.

【Feet】
Right-Kokutsudachi.

【Note】
While clenching both fists, block as if pulling them apart.

【Hands】
Right-Shuto-Gedan-Uchikomi (back of hand facing downward). Left-palm-Jyodan-Nagashiuke above the right shoulder (back of hand facing outside).

【Feet】
Pivoting on the right foot, move into Left Zenkutsudachi.

【Hands】
Stretch left fist downward. Pull back right fist to right hip.

【Feet】
Pull left foot to the right foot slightly. Stand naturally, with left foot in front.

【Note】
Do slowly.

【手の動作】
右手刀を右肩上、左手刀を下段にもっていく。

【足の動作】
右脚を軸に腰を左転し、左足を進める。

【手の動作】
右手刀上段横回し打ち。左掌額前上段受け。

【足の動作】
左前屈立ち（逆半身）。

【手の動作】
手はそのまま。

【足の動作】
右前蹴り。左脚立ち。

【手の動作】
左掌は右肩上、右掌（甲下向き）は左斜め下に出す。

【足の動作】
左脚を軸に、体を北へ向けながら蹴り足を引き、南へおろす。

【留意点】
途中の姿勢で止まらない。

【Hands】
Position Right-Shuto above right shoulder, and Left-Shuto to Gedan.

【Feet】
Keeping weight on right leg, twist hips to the left and advance the left foot.

【Hands】
Jyodan-Yokomawashiuchi with Right-Shuto. Left-palm-Jyodan-Uke in front of forehead.

【Feet】
Left-Zenkutsudachi (hips in reverse Hanmi).

【Hands】
Same as in ㊳.

【Feet】
Right-Maegeri. Stand on the left foot.

【Hands】
Position left palm above the right shoulder. With the back of the right hand facing up, extend right palm diagonally downward to the left.

【Feet】
Keeping weight on left leg and turning body north, pull in kicking leg and put down toward south.

【Note】
Do not stop at this point.

| 挙動23 | 挙動24 | 挙動25 | 挙動26 |

後ろ / 後ろ / 後ろ / 後ろ

【手の動作】
右拳右側面上段受け。左拳左側面下段受け。

【足の動作】
右後屈立ち。

【留意点】
両掌を握りながら互いに引き絞るように受ける。

【手の動作】
右手刀下段打込み（甲下向き）。左掌上段流し受け（甲横向き）。

【足の動作】
右脚を軸に、左前屈立ち。

【手の動作】
左拳下段に伸ばす。右拳右腰に引く。

【足の動作】
左足を右足にすこし引き寄せ、左足前レの字立ち。

【留意点】
ゆっくり。

【手の動作】
左拳（甲前向き）を右拳の上（甲下向き）に重ね、両拳右腰構え。

【足の動作】
右脚を軸として腰を左転、左足裏を右膝横に添え、右脚立ち。

【Hands】
Right fist Right side Jyodan-Uke. Left fist Left side Gedan-Uke.

【Feet】
Right-Kokutsudachi.

【Note】
While clenching both fists, block as if pulling them apart.

【Hands】
Right-Shuto-Gedan-Uchikomi (back of hand facing downward). Left-palm-Jodan-Nagashiuke above the right shoulder (back of hand facing outside).

【Feet】
Pivoting on the right foot, move into Left Zenkutsudachi.

【Hands】
Stretch left fist downward. Pull back right fist to right hip.

【Feet】
Pull left foot to the right foot slightly. Stand naturally, with left foot in front.

【Note】
Do slowly.

【Hands】
Hold both fists on the right hip with left fist (back of fist facing outside) on top of the right fist (back of fist facing downward).

【Feet】
Pivoting on the right foot, turn the hips to left. Place left foot sole lightly on the right knee.

【手の動作】
左裏拳上段横回し打ち。右拳そのまま。
【足の動作】
西へ左横蹴上げ。
【留意点】
横蹴上げの場合、上体が力み過ぎて引手が横蹴上げと同時に離れないこと。
【備考】
蹴上げ（目標中段）。

【手の動作】
手はそのまま。
【足の動作】
蹴り足を引いて左脚を西へおろし、腰を左転する。

【手の動作】
右前猿臂（左掌に当てる）。
【足の動作】
左前屈立ち。
【留意点】
左腕平行。

【手の動作】
右拳（甲前向き）を左拳の上（甲下向き）に重ね、両拳左腰構え。
【足の動作】
左脚を軸として腰を右転、右足裏を左膝横に添え、左脚立ち。

[Hands]
Jyodan-Yokomawashiuchi with Left-Uraken. Right fist same as in ㊹.

[Feet]
Left-Yokokeage toward west.

[Note]
For Yokokeage, avoid tensing the upper body too much, and that the pulled hand doesn't come away from the body when kicking.
Keage is Chudan.

[Hands]
Same as in ㊺.

[Feet]
Retract kicking leg (left) and set down toward west, twisting hips to the left.

[Hands]
Right-elbow-Enpi (hitting against the left palm).

[Feet]
Left-Zenkutsudachi.

[Note]
Left arm is parallel with floor.

[Hands]
Hold both fists on the left hip with right fist (back of fist facing outside) on top of the left fist (back of fist facing downward).

[Feet]
Pivoting on the left foot, turn the hips to right. Place right foot sole lightly on the left knee.

挙動30

(49)

後ろ

【手の動作】
右裏拳上段横回し打ち。左拳そのまま。
【足の動作】
東へ右横蹴上げ。
【留意点】
横蹴上げの場合、上体が力み過ぎて引手が横蹴上げと同時に離れないこと。
【備考】
蹴上げ（目標中段）。

北
North
西
West
東
East
南
South

【Hands】
Jyodan-Yokomawashiuchi with Right-Uraken. Left fist same as in (48).

【Feet】
Right-Yokokeage toward east.

【Note】
For Yokokeage, avoid tensing the upper body too much, and that the pulled hand doesn't come away from the body when kicking.
Keage is Chudan.

途中

(50)

後ろ

【手の動作】
手はそのまま。

【足の動作】
蹴り足を引いて右脚を東へおろし、腰を右転する。

【Hands】
Same as in (49).

【Feet】
Retract kicking leg (right) and set down toward east, twisting hips to the right.

挙動31

(51)

後ろ

【手の動作】
左前猿臂（右掌に当てる）。

【足の動作】
右前屈立ち。

【留意点】
右腕平行。

【Hands】
Left-elbow-Enpi (hitting against the right palm).

【Feet】
Right-Zenkutsudachi.

【Note】
Right arm is parallel with floor.

途中

(52)

後ろ

【手の動作】
左手刀は右肩上、右手刀（甲上向き）は左斜め下に出す。

【足の動作】
右脚を軸に、腰を左転。

【Hands】
Position Left-Shuto above the right shoulder. With the back of the right hand facing up, extend Right-Shuto diagonally downward to the left.

【Feet】
Pivoting on right foot, turn hips to the left.

| 挙動32 | 途中 | 挙動33 | 途中 |

後ろ / 後ろ / 後ろ / 後ろ

【手の動作】
左手刀中段受け。右手刀胸前。

【足の動作】
右後屈立ち。

【手の動作】
右手刀は左肩上、左手刀（甲上向き）は右斜め下に出す。

【足の動作】
左脚を軸に右足を北西へ1歩進める。

【手の動作】
右手刀中段受け。左手刀胸前。

【足の動作】
左後屈立ち。

【手の動作】
右手刀は左肩上、左手刀（甲上向き）は右斜め下に出す。

【足の動作】
左脚を軸に右足を東へ1歩進める。

【Hands】
Left-Shuto-Chudan-Uke. Hold Right-Shuto in front of the chest.

【Feet】
Right-Kokutsudachi.

【Hands】
Position Right-Shuto above the left shoulder. With the back of the left hand facing up, extend Left-Shuto diagonally downward to the right.

【Feet】
Pivoting on left foot, take right foot one step toward northwest.

【Hands】
Right-Shuto-Chudan-Uke. Hold Left-Shuto in front of the chest.

【Feet】
Left-Kokutsudachi.

【Hands】
Position Right-Shuto above the left shoulder. With the back of the left hand facing up, extend Left-Shuto diagonally downward to the right.

【Feet】
Pivoting on left foot, take right foot one step toward east.

挙動 34	途中	挙動 35	途中

後ろ:

【手の動作】
右手刀中段受け。左手刀胸前。

【足の動作】
左後屈立ち。

【手の動作】
左手刀は右肩上、右手刀（甲上向き）は左斜め下に出す。

【足の動作】
右脚を軸に左足を北東へ1歩進める。

【手の動作】
左手刀中段受け。右手刀胸前。

【足の動作】
右後屈立ち。

【手の動作】
右手刀は右肩上、左手刀は下段にもっていく。

【足の動作】
右脚を軸に腰を左転し、左足を北へ移す。

【Hands】
Right-Shuto-Chudan-Uke. Hold Left-Shuto in front of the chest.

【Feet】
Left-Kokutsudachi

【Hands】
Position Left-Shuto above the right shoulder. With the back of the right hand facing up, extend Right-Shuto diagonally downward to the left.

【Feet】
Pivoting on right foot, take left foot a step toward northeast.

【Hands】
Left-Shuto-Chudan-Uke. Hold Right-Shuto in front of the chest.

【Feet】
Right-Kokutsudachi

【Hands】
Position Right-Shuto above right shoulder, and Left-Shuto to Gedan.

【Feet】
Pivoting on right foot, turn hips to the left, facing north.

挙動36	挙動37	途中	挙動38

後ろ / 後ろ / 後ろ / 後ろ

【手の動作】
右手刀上段横回し打ち。左掌額前上段受け。

【足の動作】
左前屈立ち（逆半身）。

【手の動作】
手はそのまま。

【足の動作】
右前蹴り。左脚立ち。

【手の動作】
左掌（甲上）を前に出し、右拳を額前にもっていく。

【足の動作】
立ち方はそのままで、蹴り足を戻す。

【留意点】
蹴り足を戻しながら手の動作をする。

【手の動作】
右裏拳縦回し打ち。左拳左腰に引く。

【足の動作】
右足から北へ大きく飛び込み、右足前交差立ち（左足を右足の後ろに交差）。

【留意点】
交差立ちは右足に左足を充分に引きつける。

【Hands】
Jyodan-Yokomawashiuchi with Right- Shuto. Left-palm-Jyodan-Uke in front of forehead

【Feet】
Left-Zenkutsudachi (hips in reverse Hanmi).

【Hands】
Same as in ㊶.

【Feet】
Right-Maegeri. Stand on the left foot.

【Hands】
Extend left hand (back of the hand facing upward) and bring right fist to in front of forehead.

【Feet】
When retracting the kick extend the left hand out in front .

【Note】
Execute the hand movements while retracting the kicking leg.

【Hands】
Right-Uraken-Tatemawashiuchi. Pull back left fist to the left hip.

【Feet】
Take a long jumping step toward north, with right foot at first.Kosadachi with right foot in front (left foot comes behind right ankle).

【Note】
At Kosadachi position, draw left foot to right foot closely.

挙動39	挙動40	挙動41	途中

後ろ 	後ろ 	後ろ	

【手の動作】
右中段外受け。左拳左腰に引く。

【足の動作】
左足を南へ引き、右前屈立ち。

【留意点】
半身。

【手の動作】
左中段逆突き。右拳右腰に引く。

【足の動作】
立ち方はそのまま。

【手の動作】
右中段順突き。左拳左腰に引く。

【足の動作】
立ち方はそのまま。

【留意点】
挙動40〜41は連続する。

【手の動作】
両腕を右太腿の両側からすり上げる。

【足の動作】
左脚を軸に腰を左転、南へふり向く。

【Hands】
Right-Chudan-Sotouke. Hold left fist on the left hip.

【Feet】
Pull back left foot toward south. Right-Zenkutsudachi.

【Note】
Hips in Hanmi position.

【Hands】
Left-Chudan-Gyakutsuki. Pull back right fist to the right hip.

【Feet】
Same as in ⑥⑤.

【Hands】
Right-Chudan-Jyuntsuki. Pull back left fist to the left hip.

【Feet】
Same as in ⑥⑤.

【Note】
Motion 40 – 41 must be done continuously.

【Hands】
Scoop up hands from both sides of right thigh.

【Feet】
Pivoting on the left foot, turn hips to the left, facing south.

挙動42の解釈

◀左脚を軸として左転、後方へふり向くと同時に右膝を高くあげ、両掌は右腿左右側からすり出すようにして右拳（甲下）手首に左掌を添えて突き出す。あげた右膝頭と右手肘は拳1つくらいの間隔をとる。

Pivoting on the left foot, turn to the left. When body turns 180 degrees, lift right knee up high, and scoop up hands from both sides of right thigh, with left palm placed on the wrist of right hand (back of hand facing downward), and thrust them forward. Leave space about one fist between lifted right kneecap and right elbow.

【手の動作】
右裏突き。左掌右手首横添え。

【足の動作】
右膝を高くかい込む。左脚立ち。

【手の動作】
両掌肘立伏せ。
【足の動作】
左脚を軸に右足を南へおろし、右膝を充分に屈し、体を床に伏せ、右足前伏せ（右前屈）。
【留意点】
後足の足刀部が床面より浮いてはならない。床面に密着すること。
【備考】
4 mぐらい前を見る。

【手の動作】
左手刀は右肩上、右手刀（甲上向き）は左斜め下に出す。

【足の動作】
右脚を軸に腰を左転、北へ振り向く。

【手の動作】
左手刀下段受け（甲上向き）。右手刀胸前構え（甲下向き）。

【足の動作】
右後屈立ち。

【留意点】
やや低めの後屈立ち。

【Hands】
Right-Uratsuki. Place left palm on the right wrist.

【Feet】
Lift right knee up high. Stand on the left foot.

【Hands】
Push up with both palms.
【Feet】
Put down right foot toward south. Bend right knee deeply, then, drop the body down. Bend down with right foot in front. (Right-Zenkutsu)
【Note】
Don't lift edge of back foot from floor. Foot edge must stick to the floor.
Look to about 4m in front.

【Hands】
Position Left-Shuto above the right shoulder. With the back of the right hand facing up, extend Right-Shuto diagonally downward to the left.

【Feet】
Pivoting on the right foot, turn hips to the left, facing north.

【Hands】
Left-Shuto-Gedan-Uke (back of hand facing upward). Hold Right-Shuto (back of hand facing downward) in front of the chest.

【Feet】
Right-Kokutsudachi.

【Note】
Kokutsudachi should be slightly lower than normal.

◀右前屈、両掌は軽く地に着けて伏せる姿勢。ただし顔は4 mぐらい前方を見つめる気持ちでややあげる。

Right-Zenkutsu, both palms are touched to the floor lightly in Fuse position. In this case face is lifted up a little looking at about 4m front.

| 途中 | 挙動 45 | 途中 | 挙動 46 |

後ろ

後ろ

【手の動作】
右手刀は左肩上、右手刀（甲上向き）は右斜め下に出す。

【足の動作】
右足を北へ1歩進める。

【手の動作】
右手刀中段受け。左手刀胸前。

【足の動作】
左後屈立ち。

【手の動作】
右拳を前に出し、左拳を右脇腹にもっていく。

【足の動作】
右脚を軸とし、腰を左転、左足を東へ移動させる。

【留意点】
途中の姿勢で止まらない。

【手の動作】
左中段外受け。右拳右腰に引く。

【足の動作】
左前屈立ち（半身）。

【Hands】
Position Right-Shuto above the left shoulder. With the back of the left hand facing up, extend Left-Shuto diagonally downward to the right.

【Feet】
Take right foot one step toward north.

【Hands】
Right-Shuto-Chudan-Uke. Hold Left- Shuto in front of the chest.

【Feet】
Left-Kokutsudachi.

【Hands】
Prepare for the next move by extending the right fist to the left side, while moving the left fist to the front of the right hip.

【Feet】
Pivoting on the right foot, turn hips to the left, bring left foot toward east.

【Note】
Do not stop at this point.

【Hands】
Left-Chudan-Sotouke. Pull back right fist to the right hip.

【Feet】
Left-Zenkutsudachi (hips in Hanmi position).

【手の動作】
右中段逆突き。左拳左腰に引く。

【足の動作】
立ち方はそのまま。

【手の動作】
左拳を前に出し、右拳を左脇腹にもっていく。

【足の動作】
左脚を軸に腰を右転、西へ向く。

【留意点】
途中の姿勢で止まらない。

【手の動作】
右中段外受け。左拳左腰に引く。

【足の動作】
右前屈立ち（半身）。

【手の動作】
左中段逆突き。右拳右腰に引く。

【足の動作】
立ち方はそのまま。

【Hands】
Right-Chudan-Gyakutsuki. Pull back left fist to the left hip.

【Feet】
Same as in ㊆.

【Hands】
Prepare for the next move by extending the left fist to the right side, while moving the right fist to the front of the left hip.

【Feet】
Pivoting on the left foot, turn hips to the right, facing west.

【Note】
Do not stop at this point.

【Hands】
Right-Chudan-Sotouke. Pull back left fist to the left hip.

【Feet】
Right-Zenkutsudachi (hips in Hanmi position).

【Hands】
Left-Chudan-Gyakutsuki. Pull back right fist to the right hip.

【Feet】
Same as in ㊈.

挙動50	挙動51	挙動52	途中

⑧1	⑧2	⑧3	⑧4
	後ろ	後ろ	

【手の動作】
右中段順突き。左拳左腰に引く。

【足の動作】
立ち方はそのまま。

【留意点】
挙動49～50は連続する。

【手の動作】
右拳（甲前向き）を左拳の上（甲下向き）に重ね、両拳左腰構え。

【足の動作】
左脚を軸に右足裏を左膝横に添え、左脚立ち。

【手の動作】
右裏拳上段横回し打ち。左拳そのまま。

【足の動作】
北へ右横蹴上げ。

【留意点】
横蹴上げの場合、上体が力み過ぎて引手が横蹴上げと同時に離れないこと。

【備考】
蹴上げ（目標中段）。

【手の動作】
左手刀は右肩上、右手刀（甲上向き）は左斜め下に出す。

【足の動作】
右足を引き、北へおろす。

【Hands】
Right-Chudan-Juntsuki. Pull back left fist to the left hip.

【Feet】
Same as in ㊆.

【Note】
Motion 49 - 50 must be done continuously.

【Hands】
Hold both fists on the left hip with right fist (back of fist facing outside) on top of the left fist (back of fist facing downward).

【Feet】
Pivoting on the left foot lift right foot up to side of left knee. Stand on left foot.

【Hands】
Joodan-Yokomawashiuchi with Right-Uraken. Left fist same as in ㊷.

【Feet】
Right-Yokokeage toward north.

【Note】
For Yokokeage, avoid tensing the upper body too much, and that the pulled hand doesn't come away from the body when kicking.
Keage is Chudan.

【Hands】
Position Left-Shuto above the right shoulder. With the back of the right hand facing up, extend Right-Shuto diagonally downward to the left.

【Feet】
Retract right foot, and put down to the north.

挙動53	挙動54	途中	途中
 ⑧⑤	 ⑧⑥	⑧⑦	 ⑧⑧

【手の動作】
左手刀中段受け。右手刀胸前。

【足の動作】
右後屈立ち。

【手の動作】
右中段四本貫手（甲右向き）。左掌中段押え受け（右肘下、甲上向き）。

【足の動作】
右足を南へ1歩進め、右前屈立ち。

【手の動作】
右掌手首を右にひねり、右掌を中心に上体をひねりながら回す。

【足の動作】
右脚を軸に腰を大きく左転させる。

【留意点】
ゆっくりしない。

【手の動作】
右手をひねりながら、左拳で額前を縦に回す。

【足の動作】
左足を南へ進め、右足、左足を一線上に置く。

【Hands】
Left-Shuto-Chudan-Uke. Hold Right-Shuto in front of the chest.

【Feet】
Right-Kokutsudachi.

【Hands】
Right-Chudan-Shihon-Nukite (back of hand facing east). Left-Palm-Chudan-Osaeuke (underneath right elbow, back of hand facing upward).

【Feet】
Take right foot one step toward south. Right-Zenkutsudachi.

【Hands】
Twist right wrist to the right, and with right palm as the center axis, turn while twisting upper body.

【Feet】
Pivoting on the right foot, turn hips to the left with a big motion.

【Note】
Not slowly.

【Hands】
While twisting right hand, left fist rotates vertically forehead.

【Feet】
Step left foot toward south to make feet parallel.

挙動55	途中	挙動56	挙動57
 ⑧⑨	 ⑨⓪	 ⑨①	 ⑨②

【手の動作】
左裏拳上段縦回し打ち。右拳右腰に引く。

【足の動作】
騎馬立ち。

【手の動作】
左拳を右肩口にもっていく。右拳はそのまま。

【足の動作】
立ち方はそのまま。

【手の動作】
左拳槌中段横打ち。右拳右腰に引く。

【足の動作】
騎馬立ちで、南へ寄り足。

【手の動作】
右前猿臂（左掌に当てる）。

【足の動作】
立ち方はそのまま。

【Hands】
Left-Uraken-Jyodan-Tatemawashiuchi. Pull back right fist to the right hip.

【Feet】
Kibadachi.

【Hands】
Pull back left fist to right shoulder, keeping right fist in the same position.

【Feet】
Same as in ⑧⑨.

【Hands】
Left-Kentsui-Chudan-Yokouchi. Hold right fist on the right hip.

【Feet】
Kibadachi and Yoriashi (slide) toward south.

【Hands】
Right-elbow-Enpi (hitting against left palm).

【Feet】
Same as in ⑨①.

◀右手を右回しに逆にひねられたとき、上体を前に出しながら右手を右肩の上に、体と共に肘を中心にひねり回しながら、右脚を軸にして左回りに左足を前方に移す。

| 挙動58 | 挙動59 | 途中 | 挙動60 |

【手の動作】
右拳（甲前向き）を左拳の上（甲下向き）に重ね、両拳左腰構え。

【足の動作】
立ち方はそのまま。

【手の動作】
右下段払い。左拳はそのまま。

【足の動作】
立ち方はそのまま。

【手の動作】
左拳は大きく頭上に振りあげ、振りおろすと同時に右拳を頭上に振りあげる。

【足の動作】
右脚を軸に腰を大きく右転、左足は膝を上げてすばやく北へ踏み込む。

【留意点】
途中の姿勢で止まらない。左足は敏速に行う。

【手の動作】
左拳下段受け（甲後向き、小指側で下段受け）。右拳は右肩上。

【足の動作】
騎馬立ち。

【Hands】
Hold both fists on the left hip with right fist (back of hand facing outside) on top of the left fist (back of hand facing downward).

【Feet】
Same as in ⑨.

【Hands】
Right-Gedanbarai. Hold left fist on the left hip.

【Feet】
Same as in ⑨.

【Hands】
Raise left fist above head in a large sweeping motion, then sweep back down while at the same time raising right fist in the same way.

【Feet】 Pivoting on the right foot, turn hips to right with a big motion, and lift left knee high, then, stamp down left foot toward north.

【Note】 Do not stop at this point. Left foot must move quickly.

【Hands】
Left fist Gedan-Uke (back of the hand facing downward, blocking with the inner side of the arm. Right fist is above right shoulder.

【Feet】
Kibadachi.

When right hand is twisted to right by opponent, thrust upper body forward, with right hand on right shoulder, then, twist body with elbows and pivoting on right foot, swing left foot toward front.

挙動 61	挙動 62	途中	挙動 63

⑨7	⑨8	⑨9	⑩0

後ろ

【手の動作】
右拳落とし突き。左拳はそのまま（右拳を左拳の後ろに手首が交差するように。左手首上になる）。右拳甲外。

【足の動作】
立ち方はそのまま。

【手の動作】
両掌上段交差受け。

【足の動作】
両足を同時に引き寄せ、膝を伸ばして八字立ち。

【留意点】
交差受けは少し肘を曲げるぐらいで良い。勢いがついている箇所なので膝を強く伸ばしたり、踵を上げたりしないこと。

【手の動作】
両掌は交差したまま握りしめながら胸前におろしていく。

【足の動作】
右脚を軸に腰を大きく右転。左足を南へ移す。

【留意点】
ゆっくり。

【手の動作】
両拳胸前交差。

【足の動作】
右前屈立ち。

【Hands】
Right fist Otoshitsuki. Left fist same as in ⑨6. Cross both hands, with left wrist on top of right wrist and back of right fist faces outside.

【Feet】
Same as in ⑨6.

【Hands】
Jodan-Kosauke with both palms above head

【Feet】
Pull both feet together at once, and stretch knees to Hachijidachi.

【Note】
Kosauke should be done with a little bending of both elbows. As it is a powerful move, knees must not be overly straightened nor heels be lifted.

【Hands】
Clench both hands above head, while crossing, then, pull down in front of the chest.

【Feet】
Pivoting on the right foot, turn hips to right with a big motion, then, bring left foot to south.

【Note】
Do slowly.

【Hands】
Ryoken-Munemae-Kosa.

【Feet】
Right-Zenkutsudachi.

挙動 60 ～ 61 の解釈

◀相手の中段右前蹴りに対し、頭上より、すばやく足首を流すように下段受けし、縦拳（落し突き）にして突く（右拳甲外）。

Against Chudan-Right-Maegeri by opponent, Gedan-Uke by drifting down the ankle and thrust Tatekentsuki (Otoshitsuki) (back of right hand faces outward).

途中	挙動64	挙動65	途中
 101	 102	 103	 104
横 	横 	後ろ 	

【手の動作】
手はそのまま。

【足の動作】
二段蹴りの左足前蹴り。両足空中。

【手の動作】
蹴りをしながら右拳は胸前から頭上に振りかぶり、左拳は胸前へ軽く伸ばす。

【足の動作】
二段蹴りの右足前蹴り。両足空中。

【留意点】
気合い。

【手の動作】
右裏拳縦回し打ち。左拳左腰に引く。

【足の動作】
両足（右足前に）着地させ、右前屈立ち。

【留意点】
手足同時。

【手の動作】
右腕で下段を内から払うように回しながら左右両拳を大きく円を描いて回し、内側に交差しながら静かにおろす。

【足の動作】
右脚を軸に体を右回り、左足を東へ移す。

【Hands】
Same as in ⑩.

【Feet】
Left-Maegeri. Both feet in the air.

【Hands】
While executing Nidangeri, swing right fist from chest to above head and stretch left fist lightly in front of the chest.

【Feet】
Right-Maegeri. Both feet in the air.

【Note】
Kiai point

【Hands】
Right-Uraken-Tatemawashiuchi. Pull back left fist to the left hip.

【Feet】
Land with both feet (right foot in front). Right-Zenkutsudachi

【Note】
Right- Zenkutsudachi and Right-Uraken- Tatemawashiuchi should be performed at the same time.

【Hands】
Turn right arm from Gedan in a sweeping motion from inside, draw a large circle with both fists, then, after crossing inward, drop hands slowly

【Feet】
Pivoting on the right foot turn body to the right, then move left foot toward east.

挙動 62 の解釈

◀上段交差受けをした後、両掌を中心に体を右に回し相手の手首をつかんで両手をさげ、右肩で相手の逆をとる。

After blocking with Jyodan-Kosauke, turn body to right with both palms on the center line. Pull down hands, while grabbing opponent's right wrist, then, apply "Gyaku" to his upper arm with right shoulder.

左に同じ。　　　左に同じ。　　　左に同じ。　　　左に同じ。

The explanation of the move is in 104.

止め	直立	礼	直立
⑩⑨	⑩⑩	⑩⑪	⑩⑫

【手の動作】
両拳を大腿部前にもっていく。

【足の動作】
八字立ち。

【留意点】
止めの時残心に心がける。

【手の動作】
両手は開いて大腿部両側につけて伸ばす。

【足の動作】
左足、右足の順に閉じ、結び立ち。

※礼をする。

【手の動作】
手はそのまま。

【足の動作】
立ち方はそのまま。

【Hands】
Move both fists to the front of the thighs.

【Feet】
Hachijidachi.

【Note】
At Yame position, a state of alertness is important.

【Hands】
Open both hands and stretch them along both thighs respectively.

【Feet】
Move the left foot, then the right foot, into Musubidachi.

※ Bow (Rei).

【Hands】
Same as in ⑩.

【Feet】
Same as in ⑩.

抜塞大
Bassai Dai
（42 挙動）

松涛館流では、抜塞には大、小の2種類がある。抜塞大は観空大とともに流派を代表する形である。基本形を習得してから、必ず習得すべき形とされている。抜塞という言葉のとおり要塞を突き破るような気魄があり、力強く重厚な形である。受けからの受け返しが多いことから、不利な立場を有利にかえる技、力強い技、多くの変化技がある。

Shotokan-Ryu has two types of Bassai: Dai and Sho. Like Kanku Dai, Bassai Dai is one of the Kata that is most representative of the school. The general opinion is that after one has finished learning the Kihon Kata, one should be certain to learn the Bassai Dai. As the term bassai indicates, the vigor of this Kata is similar to the exertion of forcing one's way into a fortified stronghold, giving this Kata power and solidity. Because it has many Uke Kaeshis after Ukes, this Kata features Wazas that turn a disadvantageous situation into a favorable one, forceful Wazas, and many Henka Wazas.

抜塞大　挙動一覧

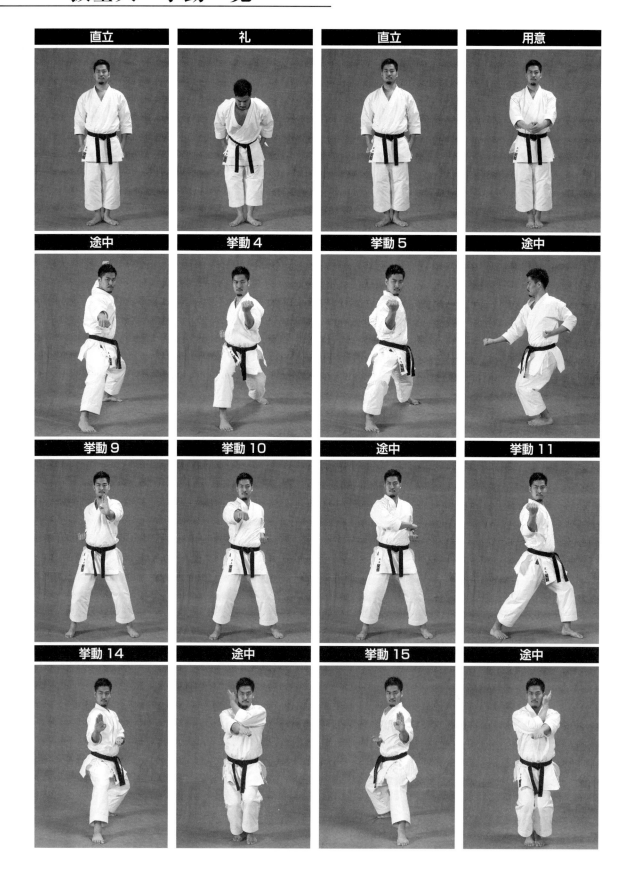

抜塞大　各挙動解説

直立	礼	直立	用意
 ①	 ②	 ③	 ④

【手の動作】
両手は開いて大腿部両側につけて伸ばす。

【足の動作】
結び立ち（左右とも正面に対して約30度）。

※礼をする。

【手の動作】
手はそのまま。

【足の動作】
立ち方はそのまま。

【手の動作】
右拳を左掌で包み、下腹部前に構える。

【足の動作】
結び立ちから閉足立ちになる。

【Hands】
Open both hands and stretch the arms down to the sides of the thighs.

【Feet】
Musubidachi (left and right feet are angled approximately 30 degrees from front).

※ Bow (Rei).

【Hands】
Same as in ❶.

【Feet】
Same as in ❶.

【Hands】
Hold right fist in the palm of left hand, and position in front of abdomen.

【Feet】
Move from Musubidachi to Heisokudachi.

途中	挙動1	挙動2	挙動3

❺	❻	❼	❽
		後ろ 	後ろ 

【手の動作】
両腕を左腰横にもっていく。

【手の動作】
右中段外受け。左掌は右手首横に添える。

【足の動作】
右足から南へ一歩半飛び込み、右足前交差立ち。

【留意点】
上体は半身。交差立ちの両大腿部は締めて、隙間をあけない。

【手の動作】
左中段外受け。右拳は右腰に引く。

【足の動作】
右脚を軸にして腰を左に回転させて北へ向き、左足を一歩進め、左前屈立ち（半身）。

【手の動作】
右拳を左脇腹にもっていき、両腕を交差して右中段外受け。左拳は左腰に引く。

【足の動作】
立ち方はそのまま（逆半身）。

【留意点】
腰をきり、逆半身になる。挙動2～3は連続する。

【Hands】
Bring both arms to the side of left hip.

【Hands】
Right-Chudan-Sotouke. Left palm is aligned with right wrist.

【Feet】
With right foot jump one and a half paces Southward, into Right Zenkousadachi.

【Note】
Body is in 'hanmi' position. Thighs should be tightly closed in Kousadachi, leaving no gap between the legs.

【Hands】
Left-Chudan-Sotouke. Pull back right fist to the right hip.

【Feet】
Keeping center of gravity on right foot, turn the body left to face North, Left-Zenkutsudachi(hips in Hanmi position).

【Hands】
Bring right fist to left side of body, then crossing both arms Right Chudan-Sotouke. Pull left fist to left hip.

【Feet】
Same as in ❼ (hips in reverse Hanmi).

【Note】
Twisting the hips, body is set in reverse Hanmi. Motion 2-3 must be done continuously.

◀相手の攻撃を押さえながら受ける。

Intercept opponent's attack while pressing down to block.

挙動1の解釈

◀相手の攻撃を受け、直ちに反撃する相手に対応するため受け替える。

Blocking opponent's attack, react to opponent's second attack by changing blocking hand.

挙動2～3の解釈

途中	挙動4	挙動5	途中

⑨	⑩	⑪	⑫

【手の動作】
左拳を左肩上、右拳を前に出す。

【足の動作】
左脚を軸にして、腰を右に回転し南へ向きながら右足を西に移す。

【手の動作】
左中段内受け。右拳は右腰に引く。

【足の動作】
右前屈立ち(逆半身)。

【手の動作】
右拳を左脇腹にもっていき、両腕を交差して右中段外受け。左拳は左腰に引く。

【足の動作】
立ち方はそのまま(半身)。

【留意点】
腰をきり、半身になる。挙動4〜5は連続する。

【手の動作】
右拳親指側手首(甲下向き)で右下段すくい受け。左拳はそのまま。

【足の動作】
左脚を軸にして腰を右に回転し西へ向きながら、左足に右足を引きつける。

【留意点】
ゆっくり。途中の姿勢で止まらない。

【Hands】
Left fist is above left shoulder, right fist is half out in front.

【Feet】
Keeping center of gravity on left foot, turn the body right to face south, moving into Right-Zenkutsudachi.

【Hands】
Left-Chudan-Uchiuke. Pull back right fist to the right hip.

【Feet】
Right-Zenkutsudachi (hips in reverse Hanmi).

【Hands】
Bring right fist to left side of body, then crossing both arms Right-Chudan-Sotouke. Pull back left fist to the left hip.

【Feet】
Same as in ⑩ (hips in Hanmi position).

【Note】
Twisting the hips, body is set in Hanmi. Motion 4 – 5 must be done continuously.

【Hands】
Using the thumb side of wrist (back of the hand facing down), Right-Gedan-Sukuiuke (scooping block).

【Feet】
Keeping balance on left foot, rotate the body right to face west and draw right foot to left foot.

【Note】
Do slowly. Do not stop at this point.

| 途中 | 挙動6 | 挙動7 | 挙動8 |

⑬　　　　　　　⑭　　　　　　　⑮　　　　　　　⑯

【手の動作】
左拳を前に出し、右拳を右肩上にもっていく。

【足の動作】
左脚を軸に右足を前に進める。

【留意点】
途中の姿勢で止まらない。

【手の動作】
右中段内受け。左拳は左腰に引く。

【足の動作】
右前屈立ち（半身）。

【手の動作】
左拳を右脇腹にもっていき、両腕を交差し、左中段外受け。右拳は右腰に引く。

【足の動作】
立ち方はそのまま（逆半身）。

【留意点】
腰をきり、逆半身になる。挙動6～7は連続する。

【手の動作】
左拳（甲前向き）を右拳の上（甲下向き）に重ね、両拳右腰構え。

【足の動作】
右脚を軸にして正面を向き、八字立ち。

【留意点】
膝は軽く伸ばす。

【Hands】
Extend left fist out in front, bring right fist to above right shoulder.

【Feet】
Keeping weight on left foot, advance with right foot.

【Note】
Do not stop at this point.

【Hands】
Right-Chudan-Uchiuke. Pull back left fist to the left hip.

【Feet】
Right-Zenkutsudachi (hips in Hanmi position).

【Hands】
Bring left fist to right side of body, then crossing both arms Left-Chudan-Sotouke. Pull right fist to right hip.

【Feet】
Same as in ⑭ (hips in reverse Hanmi).

【Note】
Twisting the hips, body is set in reverse Hanmi. Motion 6 - 7 must be done continuously.

【Hands】
Hold both fists on the right hip with left fist (back of fist facing outside) on top of the right fist (back of fist facing downward).

【Feet】
Keeping weight on right leg, turn to face front, into Hachijidachi.

【Note】
Knees should be slightly bent.

◀中段蹴りを右下段すくい受けで、大きくはねあげる。

Block opponent's Chudangeri by scooping (Sukuiuke) and throwing opponent off feet.

挙動6の解釈

挙動9	挙動10	途中	挙動11

⑰	⑱	⑲	⑳

【手の動作】
左拳を開き、ゆっくり大きく弧を描いて前に出し左中段縦手刀受け。右拳はそのまま。

【足の動作】
立ち方はそのまま。

【留意点】
ゆっくり。

【手の動作】
右中段突き。左拳は左腰に引く。

【足の動作】
立ち方はそのまま。

【手の動作】
右拳を左脇腹にもっていく。左拳はそのまま。

【足の動作】
立ち方はそのまま。

【手の動作】
右中段外受け。左拳はそのまま。

【足の動作】
八字立ちより足の位置そのままで腰を左転し、左膝屈。

【留意点】
膝屈を正確に。両足が床面に密着すること（特に後足刀部）。

【Hands】
Open left hand, drawing out a big arc extend out in front and execute Left-Chudan-Tateshutouke. Keep right fist in same position as ⑯.

【Feet】
Same as in ⑯.

【Note】
Do slowly.

【Hands】
Right-Chudantsuki. Pull back left fist to the left hip.

【Feet】
Same as in ⑯.

【Hands】
Bring right fist to left side of the body. Keep left fist in the same position as ⑱.

【Feet】
Same as in ⑯.

【Hands】
Right-Chudan-Sotouke. Keep left fist same as in ⑱.

【Feet】
Twist hips to the left without changing location of feet. Bend left knee(Left-Hizakutsu).

【Note】
Bend the knee correctly. Both feet must stick to the floor firmly (especially the edge of back foot).

挙動12	途中	挙動13	途中
㉑	㉒	㉓	㉔

【手の動作】
左中段突き。右拳は右腰に引く。

【足の動作】
八字立ち。

【手の動作】
左拳を右脇腹にもっていく。右拳はそのまま。

【足の動作】
立ち方はそのまま。

【手の動作】
左中段外受け。右拳はそのまま。

【足の動作】
八字立ちより足の位置そのままで腰を右転し、右膝屈。

【留意点】
膝屈を正確に。両足が床面に密着すること（特に後足刀部）。

【手の動作】
右手刀は左肩上、左手刀（甲上向き）は右斜め下に出す。

【足の動作】
左脚を軸に腰を左に回転し右足を南へ進める。

【Hands】
Left-Chudantsuki. Pull back right fist to the right hip.

【Feet】
Hachijidachi.

【Hands】
Bring left fist to right side of the body. Keep right fist in the same position as ㉑.

【Feet】
Same as in ㉑.

【Hands】
Left-Chudan-Sotouke. Keep right fist same as in ㉑.

【Feet】
Twist hips to the right without changing location of feet. Bend right knee (Right-Hizakutsu).

【Note】
Bend the knee correctly. Both feet must stick to the floor firmly (especially the edge of back foot).

【Hands】
Position Right-Shuto above the left shoulder. With the back of the left hand facing up, extend Left-Shuto diagonally downward to the right.

【Feet】
Keeping weight on left leg, turn body left and step South with right leg.

| 挙動14 | 途中 | 挙動15 | 途中 |

㉕　　　　　　　　　㉖　　　　　　　　　㉗　　　　　　　　　㉘

【手の動作】
右手刀中段受け。左手刀胸前。

【足の動作】
左後屈立ち。

【手の動作】
左手刀は右肩上、右手刀（甲上向き）は左斜め下に出す。

【足の動作】
左足を南へ1歩進める。

【手の動作】
左手刀中段受け。右手刀胸前。

【足の動作】
右後屈立ち。

【手の動作】
右手刀は左肩上、左手刀（甲上向き）は右斜め下に出す。

【足の動作】
右足を南へ1歩進める。

【Hands】
Right-Shuto-Chudan-Uke. Hold Left-Shuto in front of the chest.

【Feet】
Left-Kokutsudachi.

【Hands】
Position Left-Shuto above the right shoulder. With the back of the right hand facing up, extend Right-Shuto diagonally downward to the left.

【Feet】
Take left foot one step toward south.

【Hands】
Left-Shuto-Chudan-Uke. Hold Right-Shuto in front of the chest.

【Feet】
Right-Kokutsudachi.

【Hands】
Position Right-Shuto above the left shoulder. With the back of the left hand facing up, extend Left-Shuto diagonally downward to the right.

【Feet】
Take right foot one step toward south.

【手の動作】
右手刀中段受け。左手刀胸前。

【足の動作】
左後屈立ち。

【手の動作】
左手刀は右肩上、右手刀（甲上向き）は左斜め下に出す。

【足の動作】
右足を北へ1歩引く。

【手の動作】
左手刀中段受け。右手刀胸前。

【足の動作】
右後屈立ち。

【手の動作】
左手刀はそのままにして右掌を左肘下から右肩を前に押し出すように弧を描く。

【足の動作】
右脚を軸として左足を東へ移す。

【留意点】
ゆっくり。

[Hands]
Right-Shuto-Chudan-Uke. Hold Left-Shuto in front of the chest.

[Feet]
Left-Kokutsudachi.

[Hands]
Position Left-Shuto above the right shoulder. With the back of the right hand facing up, extend Right-Shuto diagonally downward to the left.

[Feet]
Take one step towards North with right foot.

[Hands]
Left-Shuto-Chudan-Uke. Hold Right-Shuto in front of the chest.

[Feet]
Right-Kokutsudachi.

[Hands]
Keeping Left-Shuto as it is, draw an arc from under left elbow to in front of right shoulder with right open hand.

[Feet]
Keeping weight on right leg, move left leg toward east.

[Note]
Do slowly.

挙動 18	途中	挙動 19	途中
㉝	㉞	㉟	㊱

後ろ

【手の動作】
右掌つかみ受け。左手刀の指先を右手首に添える。（両掌つかみ受け）。

【足の動作】
左脚前屈。

【留意点】
左手刀の指先は右手首。両肘はやや曲げる。

【手の動作】
両手はそのまま。

【足の動作】
右膝頭を両腕の中に高くかい込む。

【手の動作】
両掌を握り、右乳前に引き寄せ、両掌つかみ寄せ（両拳甲上向き）。

【足の動作】
右足刀下段蹴込み。左脚立ち。

【留意点】
手足同時。気合い。

【手の動作】
左手刀は右肩上、右手刀（甲上向き）は左斜め下に出す。

【足の動作】
左足を引きながら、腰を左に回転し、北を振り向き、右足を南へおろす。

【Hands】
Tsukamiuke with right hand. Alight fingertips of Left-Shuto with right wrist (both hands execute Tsukamiuke)

【Feet】
Left-Zenkutsu.

【Note】
Fingertips of Left-Shuto are at the right wrist. Elbows are slightly bent.

【Hands】
Same as in ㉝.

【Feet】
Lift knee up high, bringing the top of right knee in between both arms.

【Hands】
Clench both hands and pull to in front of right side of chest as if grabbing upward (backs of hands facing upward).

【Feet】
Gedan-Kekomi using Right-Sokuto. Stand on left leg.

【Note】
Hands and feet movement are simultaneous. Kiai.

【Hands】
Position Left-Shuto above the right shoulder. With the back of the right hand facing up, extend Right-Shuto diagonally downward to the left.

【Feet】
While retracting right leg, turn hips to the left, then while looking toward north put right foot down toward south.

◀右中段順突きを左手刀中段受けで受け、左手の下から右手を出し相手の右手を両手で掴んで引き寄せながら、下段蹴込みをする。

挙動 17〜19 の解釈

【Hands】
Left-Shuto-Chudan-Uke. Hold Right-Shuto in front of the chest.

【Feet】
Right-Kokutsudachi.

【Hands】
Position Right-Shuto above the left shoulder. With the back of the left hand facing up, extend Left-Shuto diagonally downward to the right.

【Feet】
Take right foot one step toward north.

【Hands】
Right-Shuto-Chudan-Uke. Hold Left-Shuto in front of the chest.

【Feet】
Left-Kokutsudachi.

【Hands】
Connect both fists in front of abdomen.

【Feet】
Pull back right foot to be parallel with left foot.

◀ Block Chudan-Junzuki with Left-Shuto, then quickly extend right hand out from under left hand, also blocking. Then, grab opponent's right hand with both hands and pull in while executing Gedan-Kekomi.

挙動22	途中	途中	挙動23

【手の動作】
諸手上段受け（両拳甲後向）。

【足の動作】
閉足立ち。

【留意点】
両拳を軽くつける。

【手の動作】
両拳を左右に拳2つ程度開く。

【足の動作】
立ち方はそのまま。

【留意点】
両拳は素早く開く。

【手の動作】
両拳で弧を描く。

【足の動作】
右足を北へ1歩進める。

【手の動作】
両拳槌中段はさみ打ち。

【足の動作】
右前屈立ち。

【留意点】
手足同時。

【Hands】
Morote-Jodan-Uke (backs of both hands facing behind).

【Feet】Heisokudachi.

【Note】
Both fists should be lightly touching.

【Hands】
Both fists separate to the left and right, about 2 fists-width apart.

【Feet】
Same as in ㊶.

【Note】
Hands move apart quickly.

【Hands】
Draw an arc with both fists.

【Feet】
Take one step toward north with right foot.

【Hands】
Chudan-Hasamiuchi, using hammer fist with both hands.

【Feet】
Right-Zenkutsudachi.

【Note】
Hands and Feet move simultaneously.

◀諸手上段突きを諸手上段受けで受けて、相手の脇腹を拳槌ではさみ打ちする。さらに順突きで攻撃する。

挙動22〜24の解釈

挙動 24	途中	挙動 25 - 1	挙動 25 - 2
 ㊺	 ㊻	 ㊼	 ㊽

後ろ

【手の動作】
右中段突き。左拳左腰に引く。

【足の動作】
右足を北へ移し、左足を引きつけ（寄り足）て、右前屈立ち。

【手の動作】
右掌を右肩上に、左掌を前に出す。

【足の動作】
右脚を軸にして腰を左に回転し南へ振り向く。

【手の動作】
右手刀下段打込み（甲下向き）。左掌上段流し受け（甲横向き）。

【足の動作】
左前屈立ち。

【手の動作】
右拳右側面上段外受け、左拳左側面下段受け。

【足の動作】
左足を引いて右足にならべ閉足立ち。顔の向きは南向きのままで、体は西を向く。

【留意点】
手足同時にゆっくり。

【Hands】
Right-Chudantsuki. Pull back left fist to the left hip.

【Feet】
Move right foot to north, pull left foot in (Yoriashi), into Right-Zenkutsudachi.

【Hands】
Move the right open hand to above the right shoulder, extend the left open hand out in front.

【Feet】
Keeping weight on right foot, twist hips left and look south.

【Hands】
Right-Shuto-Gedan-Uchikomi (back of hand facing downward). Left-palm-Jodan-Nagashiuke (back of hand facing to the side).

【Feet】
Left- Zenkutsudachi.

【Hands】
With the right fist block Jodan-Soto-Uke to the right side, and with the left fist block Gedan-Barai to the left side.

【Feet】
Pull left foot to right foot, into Heisokudachi. While keeping the face looking South, the body faces West.

【Note】
Both hands and feet move simultaneously and slowly.

◀ Block opponent's Morote-Jodan-Tsuki with Morote-Jodan-Uke, then attack opponents sides with hammerfists using Hasamiuchi. Follow up with Junzuki.

 途中
 挙動26
 途中
 挙動27

㊾ ㊿ ㈤1 ㈤2

 後ろ
 後ろ

【手の動作】
右拳は左肩上にもっていき、左拳を斜め下に出す。

【足の動作】
左脚を軸に、腰を左転し右足を南に踏み込む。

【留意点】
右膝を高くかい込んで手足同時。

【手の動作】
右拳右側面下段払い。左拳左腰に引く。

【足の動作】
騎馬立ち。

【手の動作】
顔を北へ向けながら、右拳（甲上向き）を左肩前に、左拳（甲上向き）は開手して右脇腹にもっていく。

【足の動作】
立ち方はそのまま。

【手の動作】
左掌はゆっくり弧を描いて、左掌左側面中段掛受け。右拳右腰に引く。

【足の動作】
立ち方はそのまま。

【留意点】
両手はゆっくり。

北 North
西 West | 東 East
南 South

【Hands】
Bring right fist to above left shoulder, left fist is extended pointing diagonally down.

【Feet】
Putting weight on left foot, turn hips to the left and stamp with right foot toward south.

【Note】
Bring right leg up high, moving hands and feet simultaneously.

【Hands】
With the right fist, block Gedan-Barai to the right side. Pull back left fist to the left hip.

【Feet】
Kibadachi.

【Hands】
While the head is facing forward, bring the right fist to in front of the left shoulder, open the left hand and hold it at the right flank.

【Feet】
Same as in ㊿.

【Hands】
Slowly circle the left open hand out from under the right elbow, and execute Chudan-Kakeuke to the left hand side. Pull back right fist to the right hip.

【Feet】
Same as in ㊿.

【Note】
Move the hands slowly.

挙動28-1	挙動28-2	挙動29	挙動30

㊽ ㊾ ㊿ 51

| 後ろ | 横 | 横 | 横 |

【手の動作】 手はそのまま。 【足の動作】 左脚を軸に腰を左転し、右三日月蹴り。左脚立ち。	【手の動作】 右前猿臂。 【足の動作】 騎馬立ち。 【留意点】 右肘を左掌へ打ち当てる。	【手の動作】 右下段受け。左腕胸前構え（左拳は右手の肘前）。 【足の動作】 立ち方はそのまま。 【留意点】 左掌は動かさずそのまま握る。両甲は前向き。	【手の動作】 左下段受け。右腕胸前構え。 【足の動作】 立ち方はそのまま。 【留意点】 両肘の位置を変えない。両甲は前向き。

【Hands】
Same as in ㊽.

【Feet】
Pivoting on the left leg, execute Right-Mikazukigeri while rotating the hips counter-clockwise. Stand on the left leg.

【Hands】
Right-Mae-Empi.

【Feet】
Kibadachi.

【Note】
strike left palm with right elbow.

【Hands】
Right-Gedanuke. Position left forearm in front of chest (left fist is forward of right elbow).

【Feet】
Same as in ㊾.

【Note】
Close left open hand palm without changing its position. Backs of both fists face forward.

【Hands】
Left-Gedanuke. Position right forearm in front of chest.

【Feet】
Same as in ㊾.

【Note】
Position of elbows must not change. Backs of both fists face forward.

◀三日月蹴りで相手の上段を攻撃し、右猿臂で中段を攻撃。さらに、下段を攻撃する。

Attack Jodan with Mikazukigeri, then attack with right elbow. Follow up with a strike to opponent's inner thigh.

挙動28〜29の解釈

挙動 31

【手の動作】
右下段受け。左腕胸前構え。

【足の動作】
立ち方はそのまま。

【留意点】
両甲は前向き。

【Hands】
Right-Gedanuke. Position left forearm in front of chest.

【Feet】
Same as in (54).

【Note】
Backs of both fists face outward.

挙動 32

後ろ

【手の動作】
右拳（甲前向き）を左拳（甲下向き）の上に重ね、両拳左腰構え。

【足の動作】
左脚を軸にして腰を右に回転させ、右足を少し東に出して、右脚前屈。

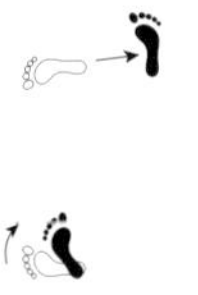

【Hands】
Hold both fists on the left hip, with right fist (back of fist facing outside) on top of the left fist (back of fist facing downward).

【Feet】
Putting weight on left leg, turn hips to the right and slightly extend right leg toward east, moving into Right-Zenkutsu.

挙動 33

後ろ

【手の動作】
山突き（左拳上段突き、右拳下段裏突き）。

【足の動作】
立ち方はそのまま。

【Hands】
Yamazuki (Left fist Jodanzuki, right fist Gedan-Ura-Tsuki).

【Feet】
Same as in (58).

挙動 34

後ろ

【手の動作】
左拳（甲前向き）を右拳（甲下向き）の上に重ね、両拳右腰構え。

【足の動作】
右足を引いて左足に並べ閉足立ち。

【留意点】
手足同時にゆっくり。

【Hands】
Hold both fists on the right hip, with left fist (back of fist facing outside) on top of the right fist (back of fist facing downward).

【Feet】
Pull right foot parallel to left foot, into Heisokudachi.

【Note】
Feet and hands move slowly and simultaneously.

挙動 31 の解釈

◀中段蹴りを右下段受けで受ける。

Block Chudan-Maegeri with Gedan-Uke.

挙動 33 の解釈

◀山突きで上段、下段を攻撃する。

Attack with Yamazuki, striking both Jodan and Gedan.

【手の動作】
手はそのまま。

【足の動作】
左膝をかい込みながら左足を踏み出す。

【手の動作】
山突き（右拳上段突き、左拳下段裏突き）。

【足の動作】
左脚前屈。

【手の動作】
右拳（甲前向き）を左拳（甲下向き）の上に重ね、両拳左腰構え。

【足の動作】
左足を引いて右足に並べ閉足立ち。

【留意点】
手足同時にゆっくり。

【手の動作】
手はそのまま。

【足の動作】
右膝をかい込みながら踏み出す。

【Hands】
Same as in ⑥⓪.

【Feet】
After lifting left knee high, stamp forward with left leg.

【Hands】
Yamazuki (Right fist Jodanzuki, left fist Gedan-Ura-Tsuki).

【Feet】
Left-Zenkutsu.

【Hands】
Hold both fists on the left hip, with right fist (back of fist facing outside) on top of the left fist (back of fist facing downward).

【Feet】
Pull left foot parallel to right foot, into Heisokudachi.

【Note】
Feet and hands move slowly and simultaneously.

【Hands】
Same as in ⑥③.

【Feet】
After lifting right knee high, stamp forward with right leg.

挙動37	途中	途中	挙動38
 ⑥⑤	 ⑥⑥	 ⑥⑦	 ⑥⑧

後ろ

【手の動作】
山突き（左拳上段突き、右拳下段裏突き）。

【足の動作】
右脚前屈。

【手の動作】
右拳を右肩上にもっていく。

【足の動作】
右脚を軸に、腰を左に回転し南へ向き左足を東へ置く。

【手の動作】
右拳を大きく振り下ろす。左拳左腰に引く。

【足の動作】
左脚膝屈。

【手の動作】
右下段すくい受け。左拳はそのまま。

【足の動作】
立ち方はそのまま。

【留意点】
肘を中心に右拳をかえす。

【Hands】
Yamazuki (Left fist Jodanzuki, right fist Gedan-Ura-Tsuki).

【Feet】
Right-Zenkutsu.

【Hands】
Bring right fist to above right shoulder.

【Feet】
Using right leg as a pivot, twist hips to the left and, while facing south, place left foot to the east.

【Hands】
Right fist swings down in a large motion. Pull left fist to left hip.

【Feet】
Left-Hizakutsu.

【Hands】
Right-Gedan-Sukuiuke (scooping block). Keep left fist in the same position as ❻⑦.

【Feet】
Same as in ❻⑦.

【Note】
Use right elbow as center pivot when returning right fist.

【手の動作】
右拳はそのまま、左拳を左肩上にもっていく。

【足の動作】
立ち方はそのまま。

【手の動作】
左拳を大きく振り下ろす。右拳右腰に引く。

【足の動作】
右脚膝屈。

【手の動作】
左下段すくい受け。右拳はそのまま。

【足の動作】
立ち方はそのまま。

【留意点】
肘を中心に左拳をかえす。

【手の動作】
右手刀は左肩上、左手刀（甲上向き）は右斜め下に出す。

【足の動作】
左足を半歩寄せ、右足を南西へ進める。

【Hands】
Keep Right fist in the same position as ❻❽. Bring left fist to above left shoulder.

【Feet】
Same as in ❻❼.

【Hands】
Left fist swings down in a large motion. Pull right fist to right hip.

【Feet】
Right-Hizakutsu.

【Hands】
Left-Gedan-Sukui-Uke (scooping block). Keep right fist in the same position as ❼⓿.

【Feet】
Same as in ❼⓿.

【Note】
Use left elbow as center pivot when returning left fist.

【Hands】
Position Right-Shuto above the left shoulder. With the back of the left hand facing up, extend Left-Shuto diagonally downward to the right.

【Feet】
Draw left foot in half a step, advance toward southwest with right foot.

挙動40	挙動41	途中	挙動42

【手の動作】
右手刀中段受け。左手刀胸前。

【足の動作】
左後屈立ち。

【手の動作】
手はそのままにして足の動きに合わせる。

【足の動作】
左脚を軸にして、右足を北西へ移し、左後屈立ち。顔は南東へ向ける。

【留意点】
顔、手足は同時。ゆっくり行う。

【手の動作】
左手刀は右肩上、右手刀（甲上向き）は左斜め下に出す。

【足の動作】
右足を半歩寄せ、左足を南東へ進める。

【手の動作】
左手刀中段受け。右手刀胸前。

【足の動作】
右後屈立ち。

【留意点】
気合い。

【Hands】
Right-Shuto-Chudan-Uke. Hold Left-Shuto in front of the chest.

【Feet】
Left-Kokutsudachi.

【Hands】
Keep hands in the same position and then match leg movement.

【Feet】
Keeping weight on left leg, move right foot toward northwest, into Left- Kokutsudachi. Face looks toward southeast.

【Note】
Head, feet, and hand movements all happen simultaneously. Move slowly.

【Hands】
Position Left-Shuto above the right shoulder. With the back of the right hand facing up, extend Right-Shuto diagonally downward to the left.

【Feet】
Draw right foot in half a step, advance left foot toward Southeast.

【Hands】
Left-Shuto-Chudan-Uke. Hold Right-Shuto in front of the chest.

【Feet】
Right-Kokutsudachi.

【Note】
Kiai.

◀相手の左中段順突きを右手刀中段受けをする。受けた右手で相手の左手を掴み北西へ引く。さらに左手刀中段受けで中段を攻撃する。

挙動40〜42の解釈

止め	直立	礼	直立
 ⑦	 ⑱	 ⑲	 ⑳

【手の動作】
下腹部前で右拳を左掌で軽く包む。

【足の動作】
右足はそのままにして、左足を引き寄せ閉足立ち。

【留意点】
用意の姿勢にもどる。

【手の動作】
両手は開いて大腿部両側につけて伸ばす。

【足の動作】
結び立ち。

※礼をする。

【手の動作】
手はそのまま。

【足の動作】
立ち方はそのまま。

【Hands】
Lightly cover right fist with left open hand, in front of abdomen.

【Feet】
Keeping right foot in the same position, pull in left foot, into Heisokudachi.

【Note】
Return to 'Yoi' position.

【Hands】
Open both hands and stretch them along both thighs respectively.

【Feet】
Musubidachi.

※ Bow (Rei).

【Hands】
Same as in ⑱.

【Feet】
Same as in ⑱.

◀ Block opponent's Left-Chudan-Junzuki with Right-Shuto-Uke, then using the same hand to grab opponent's left hand, and pull toward northwest to unbalance opponent. Follow up by attacking with Left-Shuto-Chudan-Uke.

五十四歩小
Gojushiho Sho
(65 挙動)

松涛館流では、五十四歩は大と小の2種類があり、いずれも挙動数の多い形である。五十四歩小は中段手刀受けより背手受けでの押えから縦四本貫手による三本連続中段攻撃技が特色である。これは啄木鳥が樹幹にとまり、嘴で木皮に穴をあけ虫を掘り出している様子を形に取り入れたと言われている。緩急の妙に富む形であるので、技と技の繋ぎ目が大切になる。開手技を中心とした特殊で高度な技が多くある。

In Shotokan-Ryu there are two types of Gojushiho, Dai and Sho, both of which have a large number of actions. The Gojushiho Sho is distinctive for the fact that it involves series of three middle-level attack Wazas, proceeding from a Chudan-Shuto-Uke through an Osae in a Haishu-Uke to a Tate-Shihon-Nukite. It is said that this incorporates the action of a woodpecker perching on a tree trunk, making a hole in the bark with its beak, and digging out an insect. Because the Gojushiho Sho is densely packed with fast and slow movements, the transitions between the Wazas are important. This Kata contains a large number of special, advanced Wazas, such as the Kaishu Waza in particular.

五十四歩小　挙動一覧

直立	礼	直立

五十四歩小

五十四歩小　各拳動解説

直立	礼	直立	用意

❶
【手の動作】
両手は開いて大腿部両側につけて伸ばす。

【足の動作】
結び立ち（左右とも正面に対して約30度）。

❷
※礼をする。

❸
【手の動作】
手はそのまま。

【足の動作】
立ち方はそのまま。

❹
【手の動作】
両拳を大腿部前にもっていく。

【足の動作】
左足、右足の順に開いて八字立ち。

【Hands】
Open both hands and stretch the arms down to the sides of the thighs.

【Feet】
Musubidachi (left and right feet are angled approximately 30 degrees from front).

※ Bow (Rei).

【Hands】
Same as in ❶.

【Feet】
Same as in ❶.

【Hands】
Bring both fists to in front of the thighs.

【Feet】
From Musubidachi, move the left foot, then right foot, out into Hachijidachi.

【手の動作】
右拳を額前を通るようにして大きくまわし、左拳の甲を右肘につける。

【足の動作】
左脚を軸に右足を南へすり出す。

【留意点】
ゆっくり。

【手の動作】
右裏拳上段縦回し打ち。左拳右肘下（甲上向き）。

【足の動作】
右前屈立ち。

【手の動作】
両拳を胸前で交差して、ゆっくりしぼる。

【足の動作】
右脚を軸に左足を南東へすり出す。

【留意点】
ゆっくり。

【手の動作】
両拳中段掻き分け受け（甲斜め上向き）。

【足の動作】
右後屈立ち。

【Hands】
Right fist rotates as to pass in front of the forehead, place left fist at right elbow.

【Feet】
Putting weight on left foot, slide right foot south.

【Note】
Do slowly.

【Hands】
Right-Uraken-Jodan-Tate-Mawashiuchi. Left fist is under right elbow (back of the hand facing up).

【Feet】
Right-Zenkutsudachi.

【Hands】
Cross both arms in front of chest and clench slowly.

【Feet】
Using right foot as a pivot, slide left foot towards Southeast.

【Note】
Do slowly.

【Hands】
Both hands Chudan-Kakiwakeuke (backs of hands facing diagonally upward)

【Feet】
Right-Kokutsudachi.

◀相手の突きを左拳で押さえながら、右裏拳縦回し打ちで上段を攻撃をする。

While pressing down opponent's punch with left hand, attack Jodan with Right Ura-ken Tate-Mawashiuchi.

【手の動作】
両拳を胸前で交差して、ゆっくりしぼる。

【足の動作】
左足を右足前に移し左脚を軸に右足を南西へすり出す。

【留意点】
ゆっくり。顔を南西に向けて、手足同時にゆっくり動く。

【手の動作】
両拳中段搔き分け受け（甲斜め上向き）。

【足の動作】
左後屈立ち。

【手の動作】
右拳を左肩前に出すとともに、左掌を右脇下からゆっくり大きく弧を描き前に出す。

【足の動作】
右脚を軸に左足を南東へゆっくりすり出す。

【手の動作】
左中段縦手刀受け。右拳は右腰に引く。

【足の動作】
左前屈立ち（半身）。

【Hands】
Cross both arms in front of chest and clench slowly.

【Feet】
Using left foot as a pivot, slide right foot toward southwest.

【Note】
Do slowly. Face move to south, and both hands and feet move simultaneously and slowly.

【Hands】
Both hands Chudan-Kakiwakeuke (backs of hands facing diagonally upward).

【Feet】
Left-Kokutsudachi

【Hands】
Extend right fist in front of left shoulder, and draw out a large arc from below the right armpit to the front with open left hand.

【Feet】
Keeping weight on right leg, slowly slide left foot out toward southeast.

【Hands】
Left-Chudan-Tate-Shutouke. Pull down right fist to right hip.

【Feet】
Left-Zenkutsudachi (hips in Hanmi position).

【手の動作】
右中段逆突き。左拳は左腰に引く。

【足の動作】
立ち方はそのまま。

【手の動作】
左中段順突き。右拳は右腰に引く。

【足の動作】
立ち方はそのまま。

【留意点】
挙動5〜6は連続する。

【手の動作】
手はそのまま。

【足の動作】
右中段前蹴り。左脚立ち。

【手の動作】
右中段順突き。左拳は左腰に引く。

【足の動作】
右足を前へおろし、右前屈立ち。

【留意点】
挙動7〜8は連続する。

【Hands】
Right-Chudan-Gyakutsuki. Pull back left fist to the left hip.

【Feet】
Same as in ⓬.

【Hands】
Execute Left-Chudan-Juntsuki continuously. Pull back right fist to the right hip.

【Feet】
Same as in ⓬.

【Note】
Motion 5-6 must be done continuously.

【Hands】
Same as in ⓮.

【Feet】
Right-Chudan-Maegeri. Standing on the left foot.

【Hands】
Right-Chudan-Juntsuki. Pull back left fist to the left hip.

【Feet】
Set right foot down in front, into Right-Zenkutsudachi.

【Note】
Movements 7-8 must be done continuously.

| 途中 | 挙動9 | 挙動10 | 挙動11 |

【手の動作】
左拳を右肩前に出すとともに、右掌を左脇下からゆっくり大きく弧を描き前に出す。

【足の動作】
左脚を軸に右足を南西へゆっくりすり出す。

【手の動作】
右中段縦手刀受け。左拳は左腰に引く。

【足の動作】
右前屈立ち（半身）。

【手の動作】
左中段逆突き。右拳は右腰に引く。

【足の動作】
立ち方はそのまま。

【手の動作】
右中段順突き。左拳は左腰に引く。

【足の動作】
立ち方はそのまま。

【留意点】
挙動10〜11は連続する。

【Hands】
Extend left fist in front of right shoulder, and draw out a large arc from below the left armpit to the front with open right hand.

【Feet】
Keeping weight on left leg, slowly slide right foot out toward southwest.

【Hands】
Right-Chudan-Tate-Shutouke. Pull back left fist to the left hip.

【Feet】
Right-Zenkutsudachi (hips in Hanmi position).

【Hands】
Left-Chudan-Gyakutsuki. Pull back right fist to the right hip.

【Feet】
Same as in ⑱.

【Hands】
Execute Right-Chudan-Juntsuki continuously. Pull back left fist to the left hip.

【Feet】
Same as in ⑱.

【Note】
Motion 10-11 must be done continuously.

| 挙動12 | 挙動13 | 挙動14 | 途中 |

後ろ

【手の動作】
手はそのまま。

【足の動作】
左中段前蹴り。右脚立ち。

【手の動作】
左中段順突き。右拳は右腰に引く。

【足の動作】
左足を前におろし左前屈立ち。

【留意点】
挙動12〜13は連続する。

【手の動作】
右上段縦猿臂（甲右向き）。左拳は左腰に引く。

【足の動作】
右脚を軸に左足を北へ移し、右前屈立ち（半身）。

【手の動作】
両拳を開掌し、左手刀の甲に右肘をつけ、右手刀を左肩上にもっていく。

【足の動作】
腰を左に回転し北へ向き、いったん左足に重心を置き右足を一足長分引きよせてから、右足を南へ引く。

【留意点】
ゆっくり。

【Hands】
Same as in ⑳.

【Feet】
Left-Chudan-Maegeri. Standing on the right foot.

【Hands】
Left-Chudan-Juntsuki. Pull back right fist to the right hip.

【Feet】
Set left foot down in front, into Left-Zenkutsudachi.

【Note】
Movements 12-13 must be done continuously.

【Hands】
Right-Jodan-Tate-Empi (back of the hand facing east). Pull back left fist to the left hip.

【Feet】
Using right foot as a pivot, move left foot toward north, into Right-Zenkutsudachi (hips in Hanmi position).

【Hands】
Open both hands, with left Shuto touching right elbow, and bring right Shuto to above left shoulder.

【Feet】
Turn hips left to face north and, putting center of gravity on left foot briefly, draw in right foot about one foot's length, then pull same foot towards south.

【Note】 Do slowly.

挙動 15	挙動 16	挙動 17	挙動 18

【手の動作】
右手刀中段受け。左手右肘下（甲上向き）。

【足の動作】
右後屈立ち。

【手の動作】
右背手中段押え（甲下向き）。左手刀下段受け（甲上向き）。

【足の動作】
立ち方はそのまま。

【留意点】
両手は同時。右前腕は肘を中心に手首を返す。

【手の動作】
右中段縦四本貫手（甲右向き）、左掌は右肘内側に添える。

【足の動作】
右足を北へ進め、右前屈立ち。

【手の動作】
左中段縦四本貫手（甲左向き）、右掌は左肘内側に添える。

【足の動作】
立ち方はそのまま。

【Hands】
Right-Chudan-Shutouke. Left hand is under right elbow (Back of the hand facing upward).

【Feet】
Right-Kokutsudachi..

【Hands】
Right-Haishu-Chudan-Osae (back of the hand facing down). Left-Shuto-Gedanuke (back of the hand facing up).

【Feet】
Same as in ㉕.

【Note】
Move both hands simultaneously. For right forehand, use right elbow as center pivot and turn wrist.

【Hands】
Right-Chudan-Tate-Shihon-Nukite (back of the hand facing right), with left hand attached to inside right elbow.

【Feet】
Step toward north with right foot, into Right-Zenkutsudachi.

【Hands】
Left-Chudan-Tate-Shihon-Nukite (back of the hand facing left), with right hand attached to inside left elbow.

【Feet】
Same as in ㉗.

挙動 15～19 の解釈

◀相手の順突きを右手刀で受け、背手で押さえながら中段縦四本貫手で攻撃。さらに左右連続して中段を攻撃する。

Block opponent's Junzuki with Right-Shutouke; while pushing with the back of the hand attack Chudan-Shihon-Nukite. Follow up with a left-right combination attack to Chudan.

挙動19

後ろ

【手の動作】
右中段縦四本貫手（甲右向き）、左掌は右肘内側に添える。

【足の動作】
立ち方はそのまま。

【留意点】
挙動18〜19は連続する。

途中

【手の動作】
左手刀の甲に右肘をつけ、右手刀を左肩上にもっていく。

【足の動作】
腰を左に回転し南へ向き、いったん左足に重心を置き右足を一足長分引きよせてから、右足を北へ引く。

【留意点】
ゆっくり。

挙動20

【手の動作】
右手刀中段受け。左手右肘下（甲上向き）。

【足の動作】
右後屈立ち。

挙動21

【手の動作】
右背手中段押え（甲下向き）。左手刀下段受け（甲上向き）。

【足の動作】
立ち方はそのまま。

【留意点】
両手は同時。右前腕は肘を中心に手首を返す。

【Hands】
Right-Chudan-Tate-Shihon-Nukite (back of the hand facing right), with left hand attached to inside right elbow.

【Feet】
Same as in ㉗.

【Note】
Movements 18 -19 must be done continuously.

【Hands】
Open both hands, with left Shuto touching right elbow, and bring right Shuto to above left shoulder.

【Feet】
Turn hips left to face south and, putting center of gravity on left foot briefly, draw in right foot about one foot's length, then pull same foot toward north.

【Note】
Do slowly.

【Hands】
Right-Chudan-Shutouke. Left hand is under right elbow (Back of the hand facing upward).

【Feet】
Right-Kokutsudachi.

【Hands】
Right-Haishu-Chudan-Osae (back of the hand facing down). Left-Shuto-Gedanuke (back of the hand facing up).

【Feet】
Same as in ㉛.

【Note】
Move both hands simultaneously. For right forehand, use right elbow as center pivot and turn wrist.

| 挙動22 | 挙動23 | 挙動24 | 途中 |

後ろ

【手の動作】
右中段縦四本貫手（甲右向き）、左掌は右肘内側に添える。

【足の動作】
右足を南へ進め、右前屈立ち。

【手の動作】
左中段縦四本貫手（甲左向き）、右掌は左肘内側に添える。

【足の動作】
立ち方はそのまま。

【手の動作】
右中段縦四本貫手（甲右向き）、左掌は右肘内側に添える。

【足の動作】
立ち方はそのまま。

【留意点】
挙動23〜24は連続する。

【手の動作】
両手を右肩上から腰の回転に合せて肘のスナップを使って受ける。

【足の動作】
右脚を軸に体を左に回転させ、左足を西へ移す。

【Hands】
Right-Chudan-Tate-Shihon-Nukite (back of the hand facing right), with left hand attached to inside right elbow.

【Feet】
Step toward south with right foot, into Right-Zenkutsudachi.

【Hands】
Left-Chudan-Tate-Shihon-Nukite (back of the hand facing left), with right hand attached to inside left elbow.

【Feet】
Same as in ㉝.

【Hands】
Right-Chudan-Tate-Shihon-Nukite (back of the hand facing right), with left hand attached to inside right elbow.

【Feet】
Same as in ㉝.

【Note】
Movements 23 –24 must be done continuously.

【Hands】
Block by bringing both hands from above right shoulder, using the rotation of the hips and snapping of the elbow.

【Feet】
Keeping weight on right foot, turn body left and move left foot toward west.

挙動 25

【手の動作】
左背刀下段受け。右手刀水月前構え（両甲下向き）。

【足の動作】
騎馬立ち。

[Hands]
Left-Haito-Gedanuke. Position right Shuto in front of solar plexus (backs of both hands facing down).

[Feet]
Kibadachi.

挙動 26

【手の動作】
手はそのまま。

【足の動作】
左足をそのままにして、右足を前に交差する。

【留意点】
ゆっくり。

[Hands]
Same as in ㊲.

[Feet]
Keeping left foot in the same position, cross right foot in front.

[Note]
Do slowly.

挙動 27-1

【手の動作】
右掌を上段（甲上向き）、左掌をその下（甲下向き）に両腕を伸ばして、両掌合わせ中段棒受け。

【足の動作】
左膝を左胸前にかい込む。

【留意点】
両掌の幅は顔の大きさ程度。

[Hands]
With Right hand at Jodan (back of the hand facing up) and left hand just below (back of the hand facing down) extend out both arms; combine both hands with Chudan-Bouuke.

[Feet]
Bring up left knee to in front of left side of chest.

[Note]
Distance between both hands should be about one head height.

挙動 27-2

【手の動作】
両掌を握り強く左腰に引きつけ、両拳左腰。

【足の動作】
左足を西へ強く踏み込み、騎馬立ち。

【留意点】
右拳（甲前向き）を左拳（甲下向き）の上に重ねる。

[Hands]
Grip with both hands and strongly pull both hands to left hip.

[Feet]
Strongly stamp left foot toward west, into Kibadachi.

[Note]
Put right fist (back of the hand facing up) on top of left fist (back of the hand facing down).

◀背刀で相手の蹴りを受ける。

Block opponent's kick with Haito.

挙動 25 の解釈

挙動28	挙動29	挙動30-1	挙動30-2

【手の動作】
顔を東へ向けるとともに、右背刀下段受け。左手刀水月前構え。

【足の動作】
立ち方はそのまま。

【手の動作】
手はそのまま。

【足の動作】
右足をそのままにして、左足を前に交差する。

【留意点】
ゆっくり。

【手の動作】
左掌を上段（甲上向き）、右掌をその下（甲下向き）に両腕を伸ばして、両掌合わせ中段棒受け。

【足の動作】
右膝を右胸前にかい込む。

【留意点】
両掌の幅は顔の大きさ程度。

【手の動作】
両掌を握り強く右腰に引きつけ、両拳右腰。

【足の動作】
右足を東へ強く踏み込み、騎馬立ち。

【留意点】
左拳（甲前向き）を右拳（甲下向き）の上に重ねる。

【Hands】
At the same time as looking toward east, execute Right-Haito-Gedanuke. Position left Shuto in front of solar plexus.

【Feet】
Same as in ㊵.

【Hands】
Same as in ㊶.

【Feet】
Keeping right foot in the same position, cross left foot in front.

【Note】
Do slowly.

【Hands】
With left hand at Jodan (back of the hand facing up) and right hand just below (back of the hand facing down).extend out both arms; combine both hands with Chudan-Bouuke.

【Feet】
Bring up right knee to in front of right side of chest.

【Note】
Distance between both hands should be about one head height.

挙動30の解釈

【Hands】
Grip with both hands and strongly pull both hands to the right hip.

【Feet】
Strongly stamp right foot toward east, into Kibadachi.

【Note】
Put left fist (back of the hand facing up) on top of right fist (back of the hand facing down).

◀相手の突きを両手で掴み引き寄せながら、踏み込む。

Grab opponent's punch with both hands; stamp down while pulling in.

途中	挙動31	挙動32	挙動33

途中

【手の動作】
両拳を開掌し、左手刀の甲に右肘をつけ、右手刀を左肩上に持っていく。

【足の動作】
いったん左足に重心を置き、右足を引きよせてから、右足を南へ引く。

【留意点】
ゆっくり。

挙動31

【手の動作】
右手刀中段受け。左手右肘下(甲上向き)。

【足の動作】
右後屈立ち。

挙動32

【手の動作】
右背手中段押え(甲下向き)。左手刀下段受け(甲上向き)。

【足の動作】
立ち方はそのまま。

【留意点】
両手は同時。右前腕は肘を中心に手首を返す。

挙動33

【手の動作】
右中段縦四本貫手(甲右向き)、左掌は右肘内側に添える。

【足の動作】
右足を北へ進め、右前屈立ち。

途中

[Hands]
Open both hands, put back of left Shuto on right elbow and bring right Shuto to on above left shoulder.

[Feet]
Briefly center weight on left leg, and draw in right foot, then pull right foot toward south.

[Note]
Do slowly.

Movement 31

[Hands]
Right-Shuto-Chudanuke. Left hand is connected to right elbow (back of the hand facing up).

[Feet]
Right-Kokutsudachi.

Movement 32

[Hands]
Right-Haishu-Chudan-Osae (back of the hand facing down). Left Shuto Gedanuke (back of the hand facing up).

[Feet]
Same as in ㊻.

[Note]
Move both hands simultaneously. For right forehand, use right elbow as center pivot and turn wrist.

Movement 33

[Hands]
Right-Chudan-Tate-Shihon-Nukite (back of the hand facing right), with left hand attached to inside right elbow.

[Feet]
Step toward north with right foot, into Right-Zenkutsudachi.

挙動 34

後ろ

【手の動作】
左中段縦四本貫手（甲左向き）、右掌は左肘内側に添える。

【足の動作】
立ち方はそのまま。

【Hands】
Left-Chudan-Tate-Shihon-Nukite (back of the hand facing left), with right hand attached to inside left elbow.

【Feet】
Same as in ㊽.

挙動 35

後ろ

【手の動作】
右中段縦四本貫手（甲右向き）、左掌は右肘内側に添える。

【足の動作】
立ち方はそのまま。

【留意点】
挙動 34 ～ 35 は連続する。

【Hands】
Right-Chudan-Tate-Shihon-Nukite (back of the hand facing right), with left hand attached to inside right elbow.

【Feet】
Same as in ㊽.

【Note】
Movements 34 - 35 must be done continuously.

途中

横

【手の動作】
右手刀を右肩上、左手刀を前に出す。

【足の動作】
右脚を軸に腰を左に回転し、左足を東へ移し南へ向く。

【Hands】
Right-Shuto above right shoulder, extend left Shuto out in front.

【Feet】
With weight on right leg twist hips to the left, move left foot east and face south.

挙動 36

【手の動作】
右手刀上段横回し打ち（甲下向き。外から内へ）。左拳は左腰に引く。

【足の動作】
左前屈立ち。

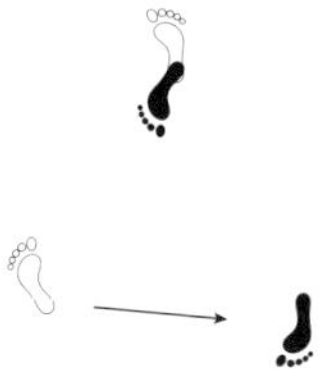

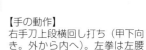

【Hands】
Right-Shuto-Jodan-Yokomawashiuchi(back of the hand facing down, arcing from outside to inside). Pull back left fist to the left hip.

【Feet】
Left-Zenkutsudachi.

【手の動作】
右手刀を左肩上にもっていく。左拳はそのまま。

【足の動作】
左脚を軸に右足を南へ進める。

【留意点】
ゆっくり。

【手の動作】
右手刀上段横回し打ち（甲上向き。内から外へ）。左拳はそのまま。

【足の動作】
右前屈立ち（半身）。

【手の動作】
右手刀はそのままにし、左手刀を左肩上に持っていく。

【足の動作】
立ち方はそのまま。

【手の動作】
左手刀上段横回し打ち（甲下向き。外から内へ）。右拳は右腰に引く。

【足の動作】
立ち方はそのまま。

【Hands】
Bring Right-Shuto to above left shoulder. Keep left fist in same position as ㊼.

【Feet】
Keeping weight on left leg, move right foot toward south.

【Note】
Do slowly.

【Hands】
Right-Shuto-Jodan-Yokomawashiuchi(back of the hand facing upward. arcing from inside to outside). Keep left fist in the same position as ㊼.

【Feet】
Right-Zenkutsudachi (hips in Hanmi position).

【Hands】
Keeping Right-Shuto in the same position as ㊿, bring Left-Shuto to above left shoulder.

【Feet】
Same as in ㊿.

【Hands】
Left-Shuto-Jodan-Yokomawashiuchi(back of the hand facing down. arcing from outside to inside). Pull back right fist to the right hip.

【Feet】
Same as in ㊿.

◀右手刀上段横回し打ちで相手の首を攻撃する。さらに手首を返して相手の突きを受け、その手で上段を攻撃する。

Attack opponent's neck with Jodan-Yokomawashiuchi. Then turn wrist to block opponent's punch, and attack Jodan.

| 途中 | 挙動 39 | 挙動 40 | 挙動 41 |

【手の動作】
左手刀を右肩上にもっていく。右拳はそのまま。

【足の動作】
右脚を軸に左足を南へ進める。

【留意点】
ゆっくり。

【手の動作】
左手刀上段横回し打ち。(甲上向き。内から外へ)。右拳はそのまま。

【足の動作】
左前屈立ち（半身）。

【手の動作】
右中段外受け。左拳は左腰に引く。

【足の動作】
立ち方はそのまま（逆半身）。

【手の動作】
手はそのまま。

【足の動作】
右中段前蹴り。左脚立ち。

【Hands】
Bring Left-Shuto to above right shoulder. Keep right fist in same position as ㊺.

【Feet】
Keeping weight on right leg. move left foot toward south.

【Note】
Do slowly.

【Hands】
Left-Shuto-Jodan-Yokomawashiuchi(back of the hand facing upward. arcing from inside to outside). Keep left fist in the same position as ㊼.

【Feet】
Left-Zenkutsudachi (hips in Hanmi position).

【Hands】
Right-Chudan-Sotouke. Pull back Left fist to the left hip.

【Feet】
Same as in ㊾ (hips in reverse Hanmi).

【Hands】
Same as in ㊾.

【Feet】
Right-Chudan-Maegeri. Standing on the left foot.

挙動40〜43の解釈

◀相手の順突きを外受けで受け、前蹴りで反撃し、右拳で相手の突きを流しながら突く。さらに相手の蹴りを下段払いで受ける。

Block opponent's Junzuki with Sotouke and counter with Maegeri, before brushing aside opponent's next punch with right hand. Follow up by blocking opponent's kick with Gedanbarai.

挙動 42	挙動 43	途中	挙動 44

61

62

63

64

後ろ（63） 　　　　　　　後ろ（64）

【手の動作】
右拳左肩前上。左拳下段突き。

【足の動作】
右膝を右胸前にかい込んでから、右足から南へ飛び込み、左足を寄せて、右足前交差立ち。

【手の動作】
右下段払い、左拳は左腰に引く。

【足の動作】
右足はそのままで、左足をやや広めに一歩北へ引き、右足は伸ばして左膝屈。

【留意点】
顔は正面を向けたまま、上体はやや斜め。挙動41〜43は連続する。

【手の動作】
両拳を開掌し、左手刀の甲に右肘をつけ、右手刀を左肩上にもっていく。

【足の動作】
腰を左に回転し北へ向き、いったん左足に重心を置き右足を一足長分引きよせてから、右足を南へ引く。

【留意点】
ゆっくり。

【手の動作】
右手刀中段受け。左右肘下（甲上向き）。

【足の動作】
右後屈立ち。

【Hands】
Right fist is above left shoulder. Gedantsuki with left fist.

【Feet】
Bring right knee up to right side of chest, then jump forward south with right foot; pull left foot into Kosadachi with right foot in front.

【Hands】
Right-Gedan-Barai. Pull back Left fist to the left hip.

【Feet】
Keeping right foot in the same position, take a deep step toward north with left foot; right leg is fully extended and left knee is bent.

【Note】
While still looking to the front, the upper body is slightly diagonal. Movements 41 - 43 must be done continuously.

【Hands】
Open both hands, with left Shuto touching right elbow, and bring right Shuto to above left shoulder.

【Feet】
Turn hips left to face north and, putting center of gravity on left foot briefly, draw in right about one foot's length, then pull foot towards south.

【Note】
Do slowly.

【Hands】
Right-Chudan-Shutouke. Left hand is under right elbow (Back of the hand facing upward).

【Feet】
Right-Kokutsudachi.

挙動 45

後ろ

【手の動作】
右背手中段押え（甲下向き）。
左手刀下段受け（甲上向き）。

【足の動作】
立ち方はそのまま。

【留意点】
両手は同時。右前腕は肘を中心に手首を返す。

【Hands】
Right-Haishu-Chudan-Osae (back of the hand facing down). Left Shuto Gedanuke (back of the hand facing up).

【Feet】
Same as in ⓸.

【Note】
Move both hands simultaneously. For right forehand, use right elbow as center pivot and turn wrist.

挙動 46

後ろ

【手の動作】
右中段縦四本貫手（甲右向き）、左掌は右肘内側に添える。

【足の動作】
右足を北へ進め、右前屈立ち。

【Hands】
Right-Chudan-Tate-Shihon-Nukite (back of the hand facing right), with left hand attached to inside right elbow.

【Feet】
Step toward north with right foot, into Right-Zenkutsudachi.

挙動 47

後ろ

【手の動作】
左中段縦四本貫手（甲左向き）、右掌は左肘内側に添える。

【足の動作】
立ち方はそのまま。

【Hands】
Left-Chudan-Tate-Shihon-Nukite (back of the hand facing left), with right hand attached to inside left elbow.

【Feet】
Same as in ⓺.

挙動 48

後ろ

【手の動作】
右中段縦四本貫手（甲右向き）、左掌は右肘内側に添える。

【足の動作】
立ち方はそのまま。

【留意点】
挙動 47～48 は連続する。

【Hands】
Right-Chudan-Tate-Shihon-Nukite (back of the hand facing right), with left hand attached to inside right elbow.

【Feet】
Same as in ⓹.

【Note】
Movements 47 - 48 must be done continuously.

途中	挙動49	挙動50	途中

⑥⑨	⑦⓪	⑦①	⑦②

【手の動作】
両手を右肩上から腰の回転に合わせて肘のスナップを使って受ける。

【足の動作】
右脚を軸に体を左に回転させ、左足を東へ移す。

【手の動作】
左背刀下段受け。右手刀水月前構え（両甲下向き）。

【足の動作】
騎馬立ち。

【手の動作】
手はそのまま。

【足の動作】
左足をそのままにして、右足を前に交差する。

【留意点】
ゆっくり。

【手の動作】
右拳は左肩前、左掌は右脇下に持っていく。

【留意点】
顔は南を向く。

【Hands】
Block by bringing both hands from above right shoulder, using the rotation of the hips and snapping of the elbow.

【Feet】
Keeping weight on right foot, turn body left and move left foot toward east.

【Hands】
Left-Haito-Gedanuke. Position right Shuto in front of solar plexus (backs of both hands facing down).

【Feet】
Kibadachi.

【Hands】
Same as in ⑦⓪.

【Feet】
Keeping left foot in the same position, cross right foot in front.

【Note】
Do slowly.

【Hands】
Bring right fist to in front of left shoulder, left open palm to under right armpit.

【Note】
Look south.

挙動 51-1	挙動 51-2	挙動 52	挙動 53

⑦③	⑦④	⑦⑤	⑦⑥

【手の動作】
左中段縦手刀受け。右拳は右腰に引く。

【足の動作】
左膝を左胸前にかい込む。

【手の動作】
右中段突き。左拳は左腰に引く。

【足の動作】
左足を東へ強く踏みこみ、騎馬立ち。

【留意点】
突きと踏みこみは同時。

【手の動作】
顔を西へ向けるとともに、右背刀下段受け。左手刀水月前構え。

【足の動作】
立ち方はそのまま。

【手の動作】
手はそのまま。

【足の動作】
右足をそのままにして、左足を前に交差する。

【留意点】
ゆっくり。

【Hands】
Left-Chudan-Tate-Shutouke. Pull down right fist to right hip.

【Feet】
Bring up left knee to in front of left side of chest.

【Hands】
Execute Right- Chudantsuki Pull back left fist to the Left hip.

【Feet】
Stamp strongly toward east with left foot, into Kibadachi.

【Note】
Punch and stamp must be performed simultaneously.

【Hands】
At the same time as looking toward west, execute Right Haito-Gedanuke. Position left Shuto in front of solar plexus.

【Feet】
Same as in ⑦④.

【Hands】
Same as in ⑦⑤.

【Feet】
Keeping right foot in the same position, cross left foot in front.

【Note】
Do slowly.

途中	挙動54-1	挙動54-2	挙動55
⑦⑦	 ⑦⑧	 ⑦⑨	 ⑧⓪

【手の動作】
右拳は左肩前、左掌は右脇下に持っていく。

【留意点】
顔は南を向く。

【手の動作】
左中段縦手刀受け。右拳は右腰に引く。

【足の動作】
右膝を右胸前にかい込む。

【手の動作】
右中段突き。左拳は左腰に引く。

【足の動作】
右足を西へ強く踏みこんで、騎馬立ち。

【留意点】
突きと踏みこみは同時。

【手の動作】
右裏拳上段縦回し打ち。左拳は右肘下に添える。

【足の動作】
左脚を軸に右足を南へ進め、右前屈立ち。

【留意点】
ゆっくり。

【Hands】
Bring right fist to in front of left shoulder, left open palm to under right armpit.

【Note】
Look south.

【Hands】
Left-Chudan-Tate-Shutouke. Pull down right fist to right hip.

【Feet】
Bring up right knee to in front of right side of chest.

【Hands】
Execute Right- Chudantsuki Pull back left fist to the Left hip.

【Feet】
Stamp strongly toward west with right foot, into Kibadachi.

【Note】
Punch and stamp must be performed simultaneously.

【Hands】
Jodan-Tatemawashiuchi with Right-Uraken. Left fist is attached to just under right elbow.

【Feet】
Putting body weight on left leg, step toward South with right foot, into Right-Zenkutsudachi.

【Note】
Do slowly.

129

| 挙動 56 | 挙動 57 | 途中 | 挙動 58 |

【手の動作】
左拳槌中段横打ち。右拳は右腰に引く。

【足の動作】
右足を北へ引き、騎馬立ち。

【手の動作】
右中段順突き。左拳は左腰に引く。

【足の動作】
右足を南へ進め、右前屈立ち。

【留意点】
挙動56～57は連続する。気合い。

【手の動作】
左拳はそのまま、右拳(甲下向き)を右腰に持っていく。

【足の動作】
右脚を軸に腰を左に回転し、左足を引く。

【手の動作】
両腕を前方へ平行に伸ばす。

【足の動作】
八字立ち。

[Hands]
Left-Kentsui-Chudan-Yokouchi. Pull back the right fist to the right hip.

[Feet]
Pull right foot toward north, into Kibadachi.

[Hands]
Right-Chudan-Juntsuki. Pull back left fist to the left hip.

[Feet]
Advance with right foot toward south, into Right Zenkutsudachi.

[Note]
Movements 56 - 57 must be done continuously. Kiai point.

[Hands]
Keeping left fist in the same position as ⑧, pull right fist to right hip (back of the hand facing down).

[Feet]
Using right leg as a pivot, turn hips to the left, pulling in left foot.

[Hands]
Extend both arms out, parallel to each other.

[Feet]
Hachijidachi.

挙動58～61の解釈

【手の動作】
両拳槌後方中段はさみ打ち（両甲上向き）。

【足の動作】
立ち方はそのまま。

【留意点】
上体を前方に倒し、尻を出すとともに、拳槌ではさみ打ちをする。

【手の動作】
両拳両腰構え。

【足の動作】
立ち方はそのまま。

【手の動作】
手はそのまま。

【足の動作】
右脚を軸に腰を強く左に回転して北へ向き、左足を移して左前屈立ち。

【留意点】
挙動59～61は連続する。

【手の動作】
両手首を交差し、ゆっくり弧を描く。

【足の動作】
左脚を軸に右足を北へ進める。

【留意点】
ゆっくり。

【Hands】
Strike Chudan-Hasamiuchi to the rear with both hammer fists (backs of the hands facing up).

【Feet】
Same as in ⓼.

【Note】
Bend upper body forward while protruding the rear, and strike Hasamiuchi with both hammer fists.

【Hands】
Bring both fists to the hips.

【Feet】
Same as in ⓼.

【Hands】
Same as in ⓼.

【Feet】
Putting weight on right leg, forcefully turn hips to the left to face north, then move left foot into Left Zenkutsudachi.

【Note】
Movements 59 - 61 must be done continuously.

【Hands】
Cross both arms at the wrists, and slowly draw out an arc.

【Feet】
Keeping weight on left leg advance right foot toward north.

【Note】
Do slowly.

◀ 後ろから抱きつかれた相手の両腕を伸ばしてはずす。伸ばした両拳で両脇腹を挟み打ちし、腰をひねって前屈立ちになりながら相手を投げる。

Break the hold of an opponent grabbing from behind by extending both arms out. Follow up by attacking both flanks with Hasamiuchi using hammer fists; twis hips and throw while moving into Zenkutsudachi.

挙動 62

後ろ

【手の動作】
両手刀を両側下段へ掻き分ける。

【足の動作】
右足前猫足立ち。

【Hands】
With both hands in Shuto, block Gedan-Kakiwake to either side of the body.

【Feet】
Nekoashidachi with right foot forward.

途中

後ろ

【手の動作】
両脇を締めて両手をやや内から外に弧を描きながら下から上へ持っていく。

【足の動作】
立ち方はそのまま。

【留意点】
ゆっくり。

【Hands】
Keeping arms in on both sides, bring hands from low to high in a slightly curving motion from the inside.

【Feet】
Same as in (89).

【Note】
Do slowly.

挙動 63

後ろ

【手の動作】
両鶏頭中段受け（両甲外向き）。

【足の動作】
立ち方はそのまま。

【Hands】
Chudan-Uke with both hands in 'Keito' (backs of the hands facing outward).

【Feet】
Same as in (89).

挙動 64

後ろ

【手の動作】
両掌は鶏頭から手首を立て青龍刀にして肘を伸ばし、両青龍刀中段打ち。

【足の動作】
猫足立ちから飛込み右足前交差立ち。

【留意点】
気合い。

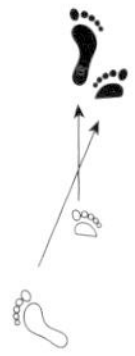

【Hands】
Change both hands from Keito to Seiryuto, by turning wrists upright, then strike Chudan-Seiryuto-Uchi.

【Feet】
From Nekoashidachi, jump into Kosadachi with right foot in front.

【Note】
Kiai.

挙動 63 ～ 64 の解釈

◀相手の蹴りを下段手刀流し受けをする。相手の諸手突きを両鶏頭で受け、青龍刀で鎖骨を攻撃する。

Block opponent's kick with Gedan- Shuto-Nagashiuke. Block opponent's Morotetsuki with Keitouke and counter with Seiryuto to the collarbones.

途中	挙動65	途中	止め

❾❸	❾❹	❾❺	❾❻

【手の動作】
左手刀の甲に右肘をつけ、右手刀を左肩上にもっていく。

【足の動作】
腰を左に回転し南へ向き、いったん左足に重心を置き右足を一足長分引きよせてから、右足を北へ引く。

【留意点】
ゆっくり。

【手の動作】
右手刀中段受け。左手右肘下（甲上向き）。

【足の動作】
右後屈立ち。

【手の動作】
両腕を体の正面で交差する。

【足の動作】
右足はそのまま、左足を引いて、両足を揃える。

【手の動作】
両拳を大腿部前にもっていく。

【足の動作】
八字立ち。

【Hands】
Open both hands, with left Shuto touching right elbow, and bring Right-Shuto to above left shoulder.

【Feet】
Turn hips left to face South and, putting center of gravity on left foot briefly, draw in right foot about one foot's length, then pull same foot toward north.

【Note】
Do slowly.

【Hands】
Right-Chudan-Shutouke. Left hand is under right elbow (Back of the hand facing upward).

【Feet】
Right-Kokutsudachi.

【Hands】
Cross both arms in front of the body.

【Feet】
Keeping right foot in the same position pull in left foot so that both feet are aligned.

【Hands】
Move both fists to in front of the thighs.

【Feet】
Hachijidachi.

| 直立 | 礼 | 直立 |

【手の動作】
両手は開いて大腿部両側につけて伸ばす。

【足の動作】
左足、右足の順に閉じ、結び立ち。

※礼をする

【手の動作】
手はそのまま。

【足の動作】
立ち方はそのまま。

【Hands】
Open both hands and stretch them along both thighs respectively.

【Feet】
Move the left foot, then the right foot, into Musubidachi.

※ Bow (Rei).

【Hands】
Same as in ⑰.

【Feet】
Same as in ⑰.

五十四歩小

五十四歩大
Gojushiho Dai
（62挙動）

五十四歩大は五十四歩小とよく似た形であり、いずれも挙動数の多い形である。五十四歩大は鶏頭より人差指一本貫手落とし突きによる3回連続攻撃技が特色である。五十四歩小と同様に啄木鳥が樹幹にとまり、嘴で木皮に穴をあけ虫を掘り出している様子を形に取り入れたと言われている。緩やかな動きから急激に早い動きへ変化するなど流れるような動きのある形である。猫足立ちによる転進や開手技を中心とした特殊で非常に高度な技が多くある。

This Kata is very similar to the Gojushiho Sho, and both Katas have a large number of actions. The Gojushiho Dai is distinguished by the fact that it involves series of three attack Wazas using an index-finger Ippon-Nukite-Otoshi-Tsuki starting from Keito. As in the case of the Gojushiho Sho, it is said to incorporate the action of a woodpecker perching on a tree trunk, making a hole in the bark with its beak, and digging out an insect. This Kata has movements that flow, such as gentle movements that change suddenly to fast movements. This Kata contains a large number of special, extremely advanced Wazas, in particular Nekoashidachi-based pivots and Kaishu Wazas.

五十四歩大　挙動一覧

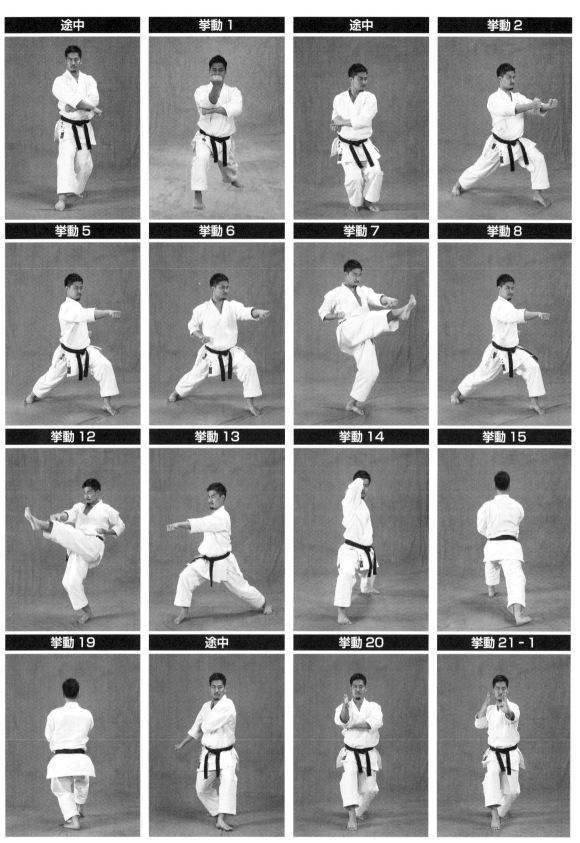

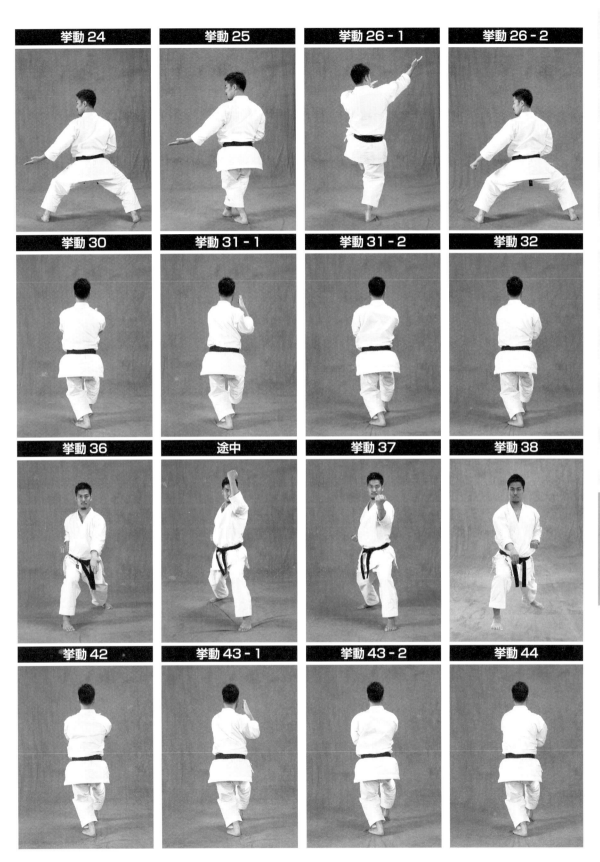

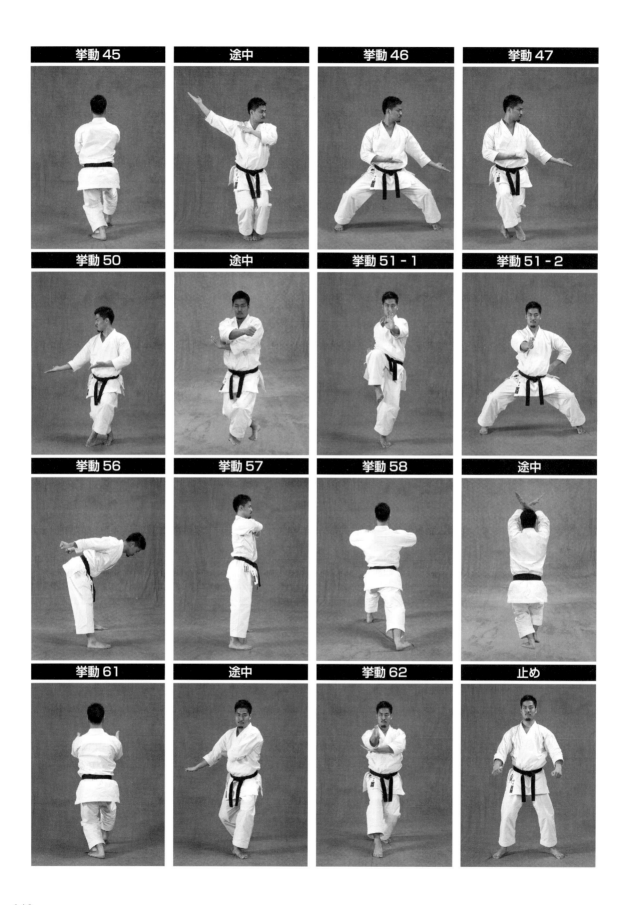

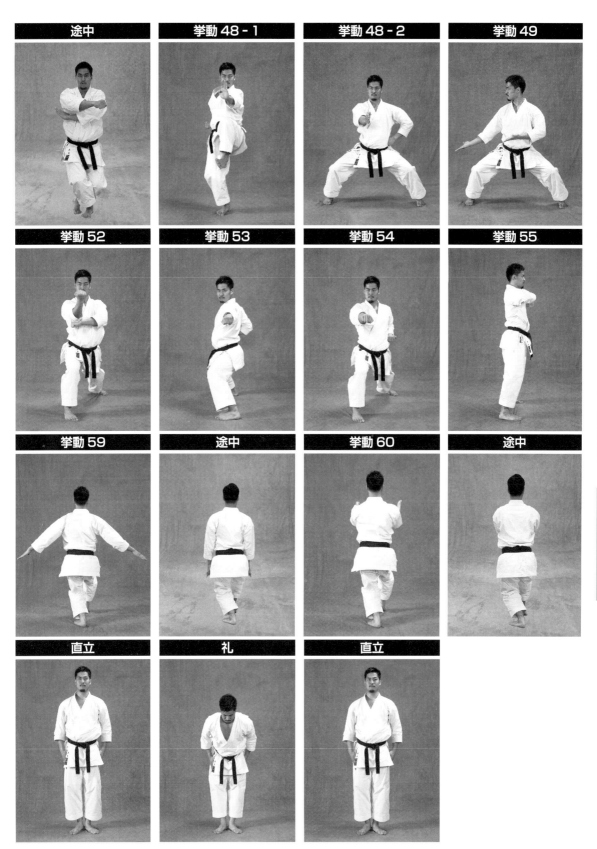

五十四歩大　各拳動解説

直立 ①

礼 ②

直立 ③

用意 ④

【手の動作】
両手は開いて大腿部両側につけて伸ばす。

【足の動作】
結び立ち（左右とも正面に対して約30度）。

※礼をする。

【手の動作】
手はそのまま。

【足の動作】
立ち方はそのまま。

【手の動作】
両拳を大腿部前にもっていく。

【足の動作】
左足、右足の順に開いて八字立ち。

【Hands】
Open both hands and stretch the arms down to the sides of the thighs.

【Feet】
Musubidachi (left and right feet are angled approximately 30 degrees from front).

※ Bow (Rei).

【Hands】
Same as in ❶.

【Feet】
Same as in ❶.

【Hands】
Bring both fists to in front of the thighs.

【Feet】
From Musubidachi, move the left foot, then right foot, out into Hachijidachi.

途中	挙動1	途中	挙動2

【手の動作】
右拳を額前を通るようにして大きくまわし、左拳の甲を右肘につける。

【足の動作】
左脚を軸に右足を南へすり出す。

【留意点】
ゆっくり。

【手の動作】
右裏拳上段縦回し打ち。左拳右肘下（甲上向き）。

【足の動作】
右前屈立ち。

【手の動作】
右拳（甲下向き）の上に左拳（甲前向き）を重ね、右腰にもっていき、そこからゆっくりと両拳を前に出して両肘を伸ばす。

【足の動作】
右脚を軸に左足を南東へゆっくりすり出す。

【手の動作】
中段諸手受け（両拳甲外向き）。

【足の動作】
左前屈立ち。

【Hands】
Right fist rotates as to pass in front of the forehead, place left fist at right elbow.

【Feet】
Putting weight on left foot, slide right foot south.

【Note】
Do slowly.

【Hands】
Right-Uraken-Jodan-Tate-Mawashiuchi. Left fist is under right elbow (back of the hand facing up).

【Feet】
Right-Zenkutsudachi.

【Hands】
Place left fist (back of the hand facing front) on top of right hand (back of the hand facing down) and bring to right hip; from there slowly extend both arms and straighten elbows.

【Feet】
Putting weight on right leg, slowly slide out left foot toward southeast.

【Hands】
Chudan-Moroteuke (backs of both fists facing out).

【Feet】
Left-Zenkutsudachi.

◀相手の中段諸手突きを下から両前腕で受ける。

Block opponent's Chudan-Morotetsuki from below with both forearms.

挙動2の解釈

【手の動作】
左拳（甲下向き）の上に右拳（甲前向き）を重ね、左腰にもっていき、そこからゆっくりと両拳を前に出して両肘を伸ばす。

【足の動作】
左脚を軸に右足を南西へゆっくりすり出す。

【手の動作】
中段諸手受け（両拳甲外向き）。

【足の動作】
右前屈立ち。

【手の動作】
右拳を左肩前に出すとともに、左掌を右脇下からゆっくり大きく弧を描き前に出す。

【足の動作】
右脚を軸に左足を南東へゆっくりすり出す。

【手の動作】
左中段縦手刀受け。右拳は右腰に引く。

【足の動作】
左前屈立ち（半身）。

【Hands】
Place right fist (back of the hand facing front) on top of left fist (back of the hand facing down) and bring to left hip; from there slowly extend both arms and straighten elbows.

【Feet】
Putting weight on left leg, slowly slide out right foot toward southwest.

【Hands】
Chudan-Moroteuke (backs of both fists facing out).

【Feet】
Right-Zenkutsudachi.

【Hands】
Extend right fist in front of left shoulder, and draw out a large arc from below the right armpit to the front with open right hand.

【Feet】
Putting weight on right leg, slowly slide out left foot toward southeast.

【Hands】
Left-Chudan-Tate-Shutouke. Pull down right fist to the right hip.

【Feet】
Left-Zenkutsudachi (hips in Hanmi position).

挙動5	挙動6	挙動7	挙動8

【手の動作】
右中段逆突き。左拳は左腰に引く。

【足の動作】
立ち方はそのまま。

【手の動作】
左中段順突き。右拳は右腰に引く。

【足の動作】
立ち方はそのまま。

【留意点】
挙動5～6は連続する。

【手の動作】
手はそのまま。

【足の動作】
右中段前蹴り。左脚立ち。

【手の動作】
右中段逆突き。左拳は左腰に引く。

【足の動作】
右足を後ろに引き、左前屈立ち。

【留意点】
挙動7～8は連続する。手足同時。

【Hands】
Right-Chudan-Gyakutsuki. Pull back left fist to the left hip.

【Feet】
Same as in ⑫.

【Hands】
Execute left- Chudan- Juntsuki continuously. Pull back right fist to the right hip.

【Feet】
Same as in ⑫.

【Note】
Motion 5 - 6 must be done continuously.

【Hands】
Same as in ⑭.

【Feet】
Right-Chudan-Maegeri. Standing on the left foot.

【Hands】
Right-Chudan-Juntsuki. Pull back left fist to the left hip.

【Feet】
Pull right foot back to the rear, into Left Zenkutsudachi.

【Note】
Motion 7 - 8 must be done continuously.

◀右中段前蹴りで攻撃し、さらに相手の右手を掴み右中段逆突き。

Attack with Right-Chudan-Maegeri, then grab and pull opponent's right hand; execute Right-Chudan-Gyakuzuki.

挙動7～8の解釈

途中	挙動 9	挙動 10	挙動 11
 ⑰	 ⑱	 ⑲	 ⑳

【手の動作】
左拳を右肩前に出すとともに、右掌を左脇下からゆっくり大きく弧を描き前に出す。

【足の動作】
左脚を軸に右足を南西へゆっくりすり出す。

【手の動作】
右中段縦手刀受け。左拳は左腰に引く。

【足の動作】
右前屈立ち（半身）。

【手の動作】
左中段逆突き。右拳は右腰に引く。

【足の動作】
立ち方はそのまま。

【手の動作】
右中段順突き。左拳は左腰に引く。

【足の動作】
立ち方はそのまま。

【留意点】
挙動10〜11は連続する。

【Hands】
Extend left fist in front of right shoulder, and draw out a large arc from below the left armpit to the front with open left hand.

【Feet】
Putting weight on left leg, slowly slide out right foot toward southwest.

【Hands】
Right-Chudan-Tate-Shutouke. Pull down left fist to Left hip.

【Feet】
Right-Zenkutsudachi (hips in Hanmi position).

【Hands】
Left-Chudan-Gyakutsuki. Pull back right fist to the right hip.

【Feet】
Same as in ⑱.

【Hands】
Execute Right- Chudan-Juntsuki continuously. Pull back left fist to the left hip.

【Feet】
Same as in ⑱.

【Note】
Motion 10 -11 must be done continuously.

挙動12	挙動13	挙動14	挙動15

後ろ

【手の動作】
手はそのまま。

【足の動作】
左中段前蹴り。右脚立ち。

【手の動作】
左中段逆突き。右拳は右腰に引く。

【足の動作】
左足を後ろへ引き、右前屈立ち。

【留意点】
挙動12～13は連続する。

【手の動作】
右上段縦猿臂（甲右向き）。左拳は左腰に引く。

【足の動作】
左脚を軸に右足を南へ移し、右前屈立ち（半身）。

【手の動作】
両拳を開き、右掌は右肩上から虎口下段押え。左掌は斜め下から下段すくい受け（甲下向き。右肘下）。

【足の動作】
右脚を軸に腰を左に回転し、北へ向きながら左前屈立ち。

【Hands】
Same as in ⑳.

【Feet】
Left-Chudan-Maegeri. Standing on the right foot.

【Hands】
Left-Chudan-Juntsuki. Pull back right fist to the right hip.

【Feet】
Pull left foot back to the rear, into Right-Zenkutsudachi.

【Note】
Motion 12-13 must be done continuously.

【Hands】
Right-Jodan-Tate-Empi (back of the hand facing east). Pull left fist to the left hip.

【Feet】
Using left leg as a pivot, move right leg toward south, into Right-Zenkutsudachi (hips in Hanmi position).

【Hands】
Open both hands; Starting from above right shoulder Kokou-Gedan-Osae with right hand. Starting from diagonally down, Gedan-Sukuiuke with left open hand.

【Feet】
Using right leg as a pivot, this hips to the left and face north, into Left-Zenkutsudachi.

挙動 16	挙動 17-1	挙動 17-2	挙動 18
 ㉕	 ㉖	 ㉗	 ㉘
後ろ 	後ろ	後ろ 	後ろ

【手の動作】
右掌は鶏頭をつくりながら、肘を中心として内側から弧を描いて前腕を立て、右鶏頭中段受け（右甲外向き）。左掌右肘下（甲上向き）。

【足の動作】
左脚を軸に右足を内側から弧を描きながらすり出し、右足前猫足立ち。

【留意点】
手足同時にゆっくり。五十四歩大の鶏頭受けは、人差し指だけ伸ばし他の四指は浅く曲げる。

【手の動作】
右鶏頭構え（右耳横）。左縦手刀を前に伸ばす。

【足の動作】
立ち方はそのまま。

【留意点】
両手は同時にゆっくり。上体をやや右にひねる。

【手の動作】
右一本貫手中段落とし突き。左一本貫手右肘内側に添える。

【足の動作】
北へ寄り足して、右足前猫足立ち。

【留意点】
一本貫手中段落とし突きはやや低めに突く。

【手の動作】
左一本貫手中段落とし突き。右一本貫手左肘内側に添える。

【足の動作】
立ち方はそのまま。

【Hands】
While forming 'Keito' with right hand, stand right forearm upright by using right elbow as a pivot and drawing an inside arc; Right Chudan-Keitouke (back of right hand facing outward). Left open hand is held under right elbow (Back of the hand facing upward).

【Feet】
Putting weight on left foot, slide out right foot by drawing an arc from inside to out, into Nekoashidachi with right foot forward.

【Note】
Both hands and feet move simultaneously and slowly.
For this kata Keitouke is formed by fully extending the index finger and bending the remaining fingers at the second knuckle.

【Hands】
Position Right-Keito next to right ear, Extend Left-Tate-Shuto to the front.

【Feet】
Same as in ㉕.

【Note】
Move both hands slowly, and at the same time. Twist upper body to the right.

【Hands】
Chudan-Otoshizuki with Right-Ippon-Nukite. Left-Ippon-Nukite is touching the inside of right elbow.

【Feet】
Move towards north using Yoriashi, maintaining Nekoashidachi with right foot forward.

【Note】
Chudan-Ippon-Nukite-Otoshi tsuki should be slightly low.

【Hands】
Chudan-Otoshizuki with Left-Ippon-Nukite. Right-Ippon-Nukite is touching the inside of left elbow.

【Feet】
Same as in ㉗.

挙動 19	途中	挙動 20	挙動 21-1

後ろ

【手の動作】
右一本貫手中段落とし突き。左一本貫手右肘内側に添える。

【足の動作】
立ち方はそのまま。

【留意点】
挙動 18 〜 19 は連続する。

【手の動作】
右掌（一本貫手）は前腕を立て、左掌の甲を右手の肘下にもっていく。

【足の動作】
左脚を軸に腰を左に回転し、右足を内側から弧を描きながらすり出し、南へ向く。

【留意点】
手足同時にゆっくり。

【手の動作】
右鶏頭中段受け。左掌右肘下。

【足の動作】
右足前猫足立ち。

【手の動作】
右鶏頭構え（右耳横）。左縦手刀を前に伸ばす。

【足の動作】
立ち方はそのまま。

【留意点】
両手は同時にゆっくり。上体をやや右にひねる。

【Hands】
Chudan-Otoshizuki with Right Ippon-Nukite. Left-Ippon-Nukite is touching the inside of right elbow.

【Feet】
Same as in ㉗.

【Note】
Motion 18 -19 must be done continuously.

【Hands】
Point straight from forearm with Right-Ippon-Nukite, and bring the back of open left hand to under right elbow.

【Feet】
Using left leg as a pivot, twist hips to the left; slide out right foot by drawing an arc from inside to out, facing south.

【Note】
Both hands and feet move simultaneously and slowly.

【Hands】
Chudan-Uke with Right-Keito. Left hand is under right elbow.

【Feet】
Nekoashidachi with right foot forward.

【Hands】
Position Right Keito next to right ear, Extend Left Tate-Shuto to the front.

【Feet】
Same as in ㉛.

【Note】
Move both hands slowly, and at the same time. Twist upper body to the right.

挙動 21〜23 の解釈

◀左縦手刀で右中段順突きを受け、右一本貫手で相手の中段を攻撃する。さらに左、右一本貫手で中段を連続攻撃する。

Block incoming Right-Chudantsuki with Left-Tate-Shuto, and attack opponent's Chudan with Right-Ippon-Nukite. Follow up with Left and Right-Ippon-Nukite strikes.

挙動 21-2	挙動 22	挙動 23	途中
㉝	㉞	㉟	㊱

 後ろ

【手の動作】
右一本貫手中段落とし突き。左一本貫手右肘内側に添える。

【足の動作】
南へ寄り足して、右足前猫足立ち。

【手の動作】
左一本貫手中段落とし突き。右一本貫手左肘内側に添える。

【足の動作】
立ち方はそのまま。

【手の動作】
右一本貫手中段落とし突き。左一本貫手右肘内側に添える。

【足の動作】
立ち方はそのまま。

【留意点】
挙動22～23は連続する。

【手の動作】
両手を右肩上から腰の回転に合せて肘のスナップを使って受ける。

【足の動作】
右脚を軸に体を左に回転させ、左足を西へ移す。

【Hands】
Chudan-Otoshizuki with Right Ippon-Nukite. Left-Ippon-Nukite is touching the inside of right elbow.

【Feet】
Move towards south using Yoriashi, maintaining Nekoashidachi with right foot forward.

【Hands】
Chudan-Otoshizuki with Left-Ippon-Nukite. Right-Ippon-Nukite is touching the inside of left elbow.

【Feet】
Same as in ㉝.

【Hands】
Chudan-Otoshizuki with Right Ippon-Nukite. Left-Ippon-Nukite is touching the inside of right elbow.

【Feet】
Same as in ㉝.

【Note】
Motion 22 -23 must be done continuously.

【Hands】
Block by bringing both hands from above right shoulder, using the rotation of the hips and snapping of the elbow.

【Feet】
Putting body weight on right leg turn body left, moving left leg towards west.

挙動 24	挙動 25	挙動 26-1	挙動 26-2
㊲	㊳	㊴	㊵
後ろ	後ろ	後ろ	後ろ

【手の動作】
左背刀下段受け。右手刀水月前構え（両甲下向き）。

【足の動作】
騎馬立ち。

【手の動作】
手はそのまま。

【足の動作】
左足をそのままにして、右足を前に交差する。

【留意点】
ゆっくり。

【手の動作】
右斜め上に両手を伸ばし、両掌斜め棒受け（両掌虎口）。

【足の動作】
左膝を左胸前にかい込む。

【留意点】
目線は両掌の真ん中。

【手の動作】
両掌を握り、左拳を左下段（甲上向き）に、右拳は腹部（甲下向き）にもっていく。

【足の動作】
左足を西へ強く踏み込み、騎馬立ち。

【Hands】
Left-Haito-Gedanuke. Position right Shuto in front of solar plexus (backs of both hands facing down).

【Feet】
Kibadachi.

【Hands】
Same as in ㊲.

【Feet】
Keeping left foot in the same position, cross right foot in front.

【Note】
Do slowly.

【Hands】
Extend both hands diagonally up to the right, Diagonal Bouuke (both hands open and in 'Kokou' position).

【Feet】
Bring left knee up to in front of the left side of the chest.

【Note】
Eyes look to halfway between both hands.

【Hands】
Clenching both fists, bring the left fist to Left-Gedan (Back of the hand facing up), and right fist to in front of the abdomen (back of the hand facing down).

【Feet】
Strongly stamp left foot toward west, into Kibadachi.

挙動27	挙動28	挙動29-1	挙動29-2
㊶	 ㊷	 ㊸	 ㊹
後ろ	後ろ	後ろ	後ろ

【手の動作】
顔を東へ向けるとともに、右背刀下段受け。左手刀水月前構え（両甲下向き）。

【足の動作】
立ち方はそのまま。

【手の動作】
手はそのまま。

【足の動作】
右足をそのままにして、左足を前に交差する。

【留意点】
ゆっくり。

【手の動作】
左斜め上に両手を伸ばし、両掌斜め棒受け（両掌虎口）。

【足の動作】
右膝を右胸前にかい込む。

【留意点】
目線は両掌の真ん中。

【手の動作】
両掌を握り、右拳を右下段（甲上向き）に、左拳を腹部（甲下向き）にもっていく。

【足の動作】
右足を東へ強く踏み込み、騎馬立ち。

【Hands】
At the same time as looking toward east, execute Right-Haito-Gedanuke. Position left Shuto in front of solar plexus (back of the hand facing down).

【Feet】
Same as in ㊵.

【Hands】
Same as in ㊶.

【Feet】
Keeping right foot in the same position, cross left foot in front.

【Note】
Do slowly.

【Hands】
Extend both hands diagonally up to the left, Diagonal Bouke (both hands open and in 'Kokou' position).

【Feet】
Bring right knee up to in front of the right side of the chest.

【Note】
Eyes look to halfway between both hands.

【Hands】
Clenching both fists, bring the right fist to right Gedan (Back of the hand facing up), and left fist to in front of the abdomen (back of the hand facing down).

【Feet】
Strongly stamp right foot toward east, into Kibadachi.

| 挙動30 | 挙動31-1 | 挙動31-2 | 挙動32 |

【手の動作】
右鶏頭中段受け。左掌右肘下。

【足の動作】
左脚を軸に右足を内側から弧を描きながらすり出し、右足前猫足立ち。

【留意点】
手足同時にゆっくり。

【手の動作】
右鶏頭構え（右耳横）。左縦手刀を前に伸ばす。

【足の動作】
立ち方はそのまま。

【留意点】
両手は同時にゆっくり。上体をやや右にひねる。

【手の動作】
右一本貫手中段落とし突き。左一本貫手右肘内側に添える。

【足の動作】
北へ寄り足して、右足前猫足立ち。

【手の動作】
左一本貫手中段落とし突き。右一本貫手左肘内側に添える。

【足の動作】
立ち方はそのまま。

【Hands】
Right Chudan-Keitouke. Left open hand is held under right elbow.

【Feet】
Putting weight on left foot, slide out right foot by drawing an arc from inside to out, into Nekoashidachi with right foot forward.

【Note】
Both hands and feet move simultaneously and slowly.

【Hands】
Position Right-Keito next to right ear, Extend Left-Tate-Shuto to the front.

【Feet】
Same as in ㊺.

【Note】
Move both hands slowly, and at the same time. Twist upper body to the right.

【Hands】
Chudan-Otoshizuki with Right Ippon-Nukite. Left-Ippon-Nukite is touching the inside of right elbow.

【Feet】
Move towards north using Yoriashi, maintaining Nekoashidachi with right foot forward.

【Hands】
Chudan-Otoshizuki with Left-Ippon-Nukite. Right-Ippon-Nukite is touching the inside of left elbow.

【Feet】
Same as in ㊼.

| 挙動33 | 挙動34 | 途中 | 挙動35 |

後ろ

【手の動作】
右一本貫手中段落とし突き。左一本貫手右肘内側に添える。

【足の動作】
立ち方はそのまま。

【留意点】
挙動32〜33は連続する。

【手の動作】
右下段横四本貫手（甲下向き）。左拳は左腰に引く。

【足の動作】
右脚を軸に腰を左に回転し南へ向き、左前屈立ち。

【手の動作】
肘を中心に右拳を額前からゆっくり弧を描く。左拳はそのまま。

【足の動作】
左脚を軸に右足を南へ進める。

【留意点】
手足同時にゆっくり。

【手の動作】
右裏拳上段縦回し打ち。左拳はそのまま。

【足の動作】
右前屈立ち（半身）。

北 North
西 West ／ 東 East
南 South

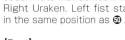

【Hands】
Chudan-Otoshizuki with Right Ippon-Nukite. Left-Ippon-Nukite is touching the inside of right elbow.

【Feet】
Same as in ㊼.

【Note】
Motion 32 -33 must be done continuously.

【Hands】
Gedantsuki with Right-Shihon-Nukite (palm facing up). Pull left fist to left hip.

【Feet】
Using left leg as a pivot twist hips left to face south, into Left Zenkutsudachi.

【Hands】
Using the elbow as a center pivot, draw an arc with right fist, starting from in front of the forehead. Keep left fist in same position as ㊿.

【Feet】
Putting weight on left foot, advance right foot towards south.

【Note】
Both hands and feet move simultaneously and slowly.

【Hands】
Jodan-Tate-Mawashiuchi with Right Uraken. Left fist stays in the same position as ㊿.

【Feet】
Right-Zenkutsudachi (hips in Hanmi position).

◀右裏拳上段縦回し打ちで相手の上段を攻撃する。さらに左下段横四本貫手で下段を攻撃する。

Block opponent's Left-Jodantsuki with rising right forearm, and strike Jodan-Tate-Mawashiuchi with Right-Uraken. Follow up by striking with Yohon-Nukite to Gedan.

挙動35〜36の解釈

挙動 36	途中	挙動 37	挙動 38

【手の動作】
右下段横四本貫手（甲下向き）。右拳は右腰に引く。

【足の動作】
立ち方はそのまま。

【手の動作】
肘を中心に左拳を額前からゆっくり弧を描く。右拳はそのまま。

【足の動作】
右脚を軸に左足を南へ進める。

【留意点】
手足同時にゆっくり。

【手の動作】
左裏拳上段縦回し打ち。右拳はそのまま。

【足の動作】
左前屈立ち（半身）。

【手の動作】
右拳を右鷲手に変え肩を中心に大きく回し、鷲手下段落とし打ち。

【足の動作】
右足を南へ進め、右前屈立ち。

【留意点】
手首のバネを効かす。

【Hands】
Gedantsuki with Left-Shihon-Nukite (palm facing up). Pull right fist to right hip.

【Feet】
Same as in ㉒.

【Hands】
Using the elbow as a center pivot, draw an arc with left fist, starting from in front of the forehead. Keep right fist in same position as ㊿.

【Feet】
Putting weight on right foot, advance left foot towards south.

【Note】
Both hands and feet move simultaneously and slowly.

【Hands】
Jodan-Tate-Mawashiuchi with Right Uraken. Left fist stays in the same position as ㊿.

【Feet】
Left-Zenkutsudachi (hips in Hanmi position).

【Hands】
Open up right hand to Right Washide and make a large circle, using the shoulder as the center; attack Gedan Otoshiuchi with Washide.

【Feet】
Step south with right foot, into Right Zenkutsudachi.

【Note】
Make use of the elasticity in the wrist.

挙動 38 〜 39 の解釈

◀鷲手で相手の甲を叩き落とすように打つ。さらに鷲手を上向きに変え相手の顎を突上げる。

Hit the back of opponent's fist with Washide, then under the opponent's jaw with a rising strike.

挙動 39	挙動 40	挙動 41-1	挙動 41-2

後ろ

【手の動作】
右鷲手上段突上げ。左拳はそのまま。

【足の動作】
立ち方はそのまま。

【留意点】
挙動38〜39は連続する。手首のバネを効かす。

【手の動作】
手はそのまま。

【足の動作】
左上段前蹴り。右脚立ち。

【手の動作】
右拳は左肩前に引く。左拳中段突き。

【足の動作】
左蹴り足を引き、右脚立ち。

【手の動作】
右拳後方下段受け。左肘上段当て。

【足の動作】
右足を軸に腰を左に回転し、北へ向き、左足を北へおろし、左前屈立ち。

【留意点】
手足同時。

【Hands】
Jodan Tsukiage with Right Washite. Keep left fist in the same position as ㊱.

【Feet】
Same as in ㊱.

【Note】
Movements 38 - 39 must be done continuously.
Make use of the elasticity in the wrist.

【Hands】
Same as in ㊲.

【Feet】
Left-Jodan-Maegeri. Standing on the right foot.

【Hands】
Pull right fist to in front of left shoulder. Left fist punches ChudanTsuki.

【Feet】
Retract right leg, standing on left.

【Hands】
Gedan-Uke to the rear with right fist. Strike Jodan with left elbow.

【Feet】
Using right leg as a pivot, turn hips to the left to face north and set down left foot toward north.

【Note】
Hand and feet movements are simultaneous.

挙動 40〜41 の解釈

◀前蹴りで中段を攻撃する。相手が上段順突きで攻撃してきたところ、右拳で流しながら中段突きをする。さらに後方からの蹴りを下段受けする。

Opponent blocks Maegeri attack; when opponent counterattacks Jodan-Junzuki, execute Chudantsuki while deflecting opponent's right fist. Follow up by blocking incoming kick from the rear with Gedan Uke.

挙動 42

後ろ

【手の動作】
両拳を開き、右掌（一本貫手）は前腕を立て、右鶏頭中段受け（右甲外向き）。左掌の甲を右肘下にもっていく。
【足の動作】
左脚を軸に右足を内側から弧を描きながらすり出し、右足前猫足立ち。
【留意点】
手足同時にゆっくり。

【Hands】
While forming 'Keito' with right hand, stand right forearm upright by using right elbow as a pivot and drawing an inside arc; Right Chudan-Keitouke (back of right hand facing outward). Left open hand is held under right elbow.
【Feet】
Putting weight on left foot, slide out right foot by drawing an arc from inside to out, into Nekoashidachi with right foot forward.
【Note】
Both hands and feet move simultaneously and slowly.

◀肘で相手の上段を攻撃する。
Attack Jodan with the elbow.

挙動41の解釈

挙動 43-1

後ろ

【手の動作】
右鶏頭構え（右耳横）。左縦手刀を前に伸ばす。
【足の動作】
立ち方はそのまま。
【留意点】
両手は同時にゆっくり。上体をやや右にひねる。

【Hands】
Position Right-Keito next to right ear. Extend Left-Tate-Shuto to the front.
【Feet】
Same as in ㉛.
【Note】
Move both hands slowly, and at the same time. Twist upper body to the right.

挙動 43-2

後ろ

【手の動作】
右一本貫手中段落とし突き。左一本貫手右肘内側に添える。
【足の動作】
北へ寄り足して、右足前猫足立ち。

【Hands】
Chudan-Otoshizuki with Right Ippon-Nukite. Left-Ippon-Nukite is touching the inside of right elbow.
【Feet】
Move towards north using Yoriashi, maintaining Nekoashidachi with right foot forward.

挙動 44

後ろ

【手の動作】
左一本貫手中段落とし突き。右一本貫手左肘内側に添える。
【足の動作】
立ち方はそのまま。

【Hands】
Chudan-Otoshizuki with Left-Ippon-Nukite. Right-Ippon-Nukite is touching the inside of left elbow.
【Feet】
Same as in ㉝.

挙動 45 / 途中 / 挙動 46 / 挙動 47

65 / 66 / 67 / 68

後ろ

【手の動作】
右一本貫手中段落とし突き。左一本貫手右肘内側に添える。

【足の動作】
立ち方はそのまま。

【留意点】
挙動44～45は連続する。

【手の動作】
両手を右肩上から腰の回転に合せて肘のスナップを使って受ける。

【足の動作】
右脚を軸に体を左に回転させ、左足を東へ移す。

【手の動作】
左背刀下段受け。右手刀水月前構え（両甲下向き）。

【足の動作】
騎馬立ち。

【手の動作】
手はそのまま。

【足の動作】
左足をそのままにして、右足を前に交差する。

【留意点】
ゆっくり。

【Hands】
Chudan-Otoshizuki with Right Ippon-Nukite. Left-Ippon-Nukite is touching the inside of right elbow.

【Feet】
Same as in ❸.

【Note】
Motion 44 -45 must be done continuously.

【Hands】
Block by bringing both hands from above right shoulder, using the rotation of the hips and snapping of the elbow.

【Feet】
Putting body weight on right leg turn body left, moving left leg towards east.

【Hands】
Left-Haito-Gedanuke. Position right Shuto in front of solar plexus (backs of both hands facing down).

【Feet】
Kibadachi.

【Hands】
Same as in ❻.

【Feet】
Keeping left foot in the same position, cross right foot in front.

【Note】
Do slowly.

途中	挙動48-1	挙動48-2	挙動49
⑥⑨	 ⑦⓪	 ⑦①	 ⑦②

【手の動作】
右拳を左肩前、左手刀は右脇下にもっていく。

【留意点】
顔は南を向く。

【手の動作】
左中段縦手刀受け。右拳は右腰に引く。

【足の動作】
左膝を左胸前にかい込む。

【手の動作】
右中段縦四本貫手（甲右向き）、左肘横張り左腰構え。

【足の動作】
左足を東へ強く踏み込み、騎馬立ち。

【留意点】
突きと踏み込みは同時。

【手の動作】
顔を西へ向けるとともに、右背刀下段受け。左手刀水月前構え。

【足の動作】
立ち方はそのまま。

【Hands】
Bring right fist to in front of left shoulder, left Shuto to under right armpit.

【Note】
Look south.

【Hands】
Left-Chudan-Tate-Shutouke. Pull down right fist to right hip.

【Feet】
Raise left foot to in front of left side of the chest.

【Hands】
Right Chudan-Tate-Shihon-Nukite (back of the hand facing right), with left elbow protruding to the side, position left fist at left hip.

【Feet】
Strongly stamp left foot toward east, into Kibadachi.

【Note】
Punch and stamp must be performed simultaneously.

【Hands】
At the same time as looking toward west, execute Right-Haito-Gedanuke. Position left Shuto in front of solar plexus.

【Feet】
Same as in ⑦①.

| 挙動50 | 途中 | 挙動51-1 | 挙動51-2 |

【手の動作】
手はそのまま。

【足の動作】
右足をそのままにして、左足を前に交差する。

【留意点】
ゆっくり。

【手の動作】
右拳を左肩前、左手刀は右脇下にもっていく。

【留意点】
顔は南を向く。

【手の動作】
左中段縦手刀受け。右拳は右腰に引く。

【足の動作】
右膝を右胸前にかい込む。

【手の動作】
右中段縦四本貫手（甲右向き）、左肘横張り左腰構え。

【足の動作】
右足を西へ強く踏み込み、騎馬立ち。

【留意点】
突きと踏み込みは同時。

【Hands】
Same as in ⑫.

【Feet】
Keeping right foot in the same position, cross left foot in front.

【Note】
Do slowly.

【Hands】
Bring right fist to in front of left shoulder, left Shuto to under right armpit.

【Note】
Look south.

【Hands】
Left-Chudan-Tate-Shutouke. Pull down right fist to right hip.

【Feet】
Raise right foot to in front of right side of the chest.

【Hands】
Right Chudan-Tate-Shihon-Nukite (back of the hand facing right), with left elbow protruding to the side, position left fist at left hip.

【Feet】
Strongly stamp right foot toward west, into Kibadachi.

【Note】
Punch and stamp must be performed simultaneously.

◀縦回し打ちで顔面を攻撃し、相手がさらに左順突きで攻撃してくるのを中段横打ちで相手の脇腹を攻撃する。下がる相手に中段順突きで攻撃する。

Attack the face with Tate-Mawashiuchi, then counter opponent's incoming Left Junzuki with Chudan Yokouchi to the side of the body. While opponent is still reeling, attack Chudan Junzuki.

挙動 52

【手の動作】
右裏拳上段縦回し打ち。左拳は右肘下に添える。

【足の動作】
左脚を軸に右足を南へ進め、右前屈立ち。

【留意点】
ゆっくり。

[Hands]
Jodan-Tatemawashiuchi with Right-Uraken. Left fist is attached to just under right elbow.

[Feet]
Putting body weight on left leg, step toward south with right foot, into Right Zenkutsudachi.

[Note]
Do slowly.

挙動 53

【手の動作】
左拳槌中段横打ち。右拳は右腰に引く。

【足の動作】
右足を北へ引き、騎馬立ち。

[Hands]
Left-Kentsui-Chudan-Yoko-Mawashi-Uchi. Pull the right fist to the right hip.

[Feet]
Pull right foot toward north, into Kibadachi.

挙動 54

【手の動作】
右中段順突き。左拳は左腰に引く。

【足の動作】
右足を南へ進め、右前屈立ち。

【留意点】
挙動 53〜54 は連続する。気合い。

[Hands]
Right-Chudan-Juntsuki. Pull back left fist to the left hip.

[Feet]
Advance with right foot toward south, into Right Zenkutsudachi.

[Note]
Motion 53 - 54 must be done continuously. Kiai.

挙動 55

【手の動作】
肘を外側に張り、両拳両乳前構え。

【足の動作】
右脚を軸に腰を左に回転し、左足を引き八字立ち。

[Hands]
Extend elbows out to the sides, and position both hands in front of chest.

[Note]
Putting weight on right leg, turn hips to the left, pulling left leg into Hachijidachi.

挙動 55〜58 の解釈

後ろから抱きつかれた両手を肘を側方に張り外し、両拳槌で相手の脇腹を攻撃する。さらに抱きつきにきた相手の両手を掴み、腰を左転し相手を投げる。
Break the hold of a rear grab by forcefully extending out elbows to the sides, then attack both sides of opponent's body using hammer fists. Follow up by grabbing opponent's hands, twisting hips left and throwing opponent.

挙動56	挙動57	挙動58	途中

		後ろ 	後ろ 

【手の動作】
両拳槌後方中段はさみ打ち（両甲上向き）。

【足の動作】
立ち方はそのまま。

【留意点】
上体を前方に倒し、尻を出すとともに、拳槌ではさみ打ちをする。

【手の動作】
両肘を水平に張り、両拳両乳前構え。

【足の動作】
立ち方はそのまま。

【手の動作】
手はそのまま。

【足の動作】
右脚を軸に腰を強く左に回転して北へ向き、左足を移して左前屈立ち。

【留意点】
挙動56〜58は連続する。

【手の動作】
両手首を交差し、ゆっくり弧を描く。

【足の動作】
左脚を軸に右足を北へ進める。

【留意点】
手足同時にゆっくり。

【Hands】
Strike Chudan-Hasamiuchi to the rear with both hammer fists (backs of the hands facing up).

【Feet】
Same as in ⑳.

【Note】
Bend upper body forward while protruding the rear, and strike Hasamiuchi with both hammer fists.

【Hands】
Extend both elbows out horizontally, position both fists in front of chest.

【Feet】
Same as in ⑳.

【Hands】
Same as in ㉒.

【Feet】
Putting weight on right leg, forcefully turn hips to the left to face north, then move left foot into Left Zenkutsudachi.

【Note】
Motion 56-58 must be done continuously.

【Hands】
Cross both arms at the wrists, and slowly draw out an arc.

【Feet】
Keeping weight on left leg advance right foot toward north.

【Note】
Both hands and feet move simultaneously and slowly.

挙動59	途中	挙動60	途中
⑧⑤	⑧⑥	⑧⑦	⑧⑧
後ろ	後ろ	後ろ	後ろ
【手の動作】両手刀を両側下段へ掻き分ける。	【手の動作】両脇を締めて両手をやや内から外に弧を描きながら下から上へ持っていく。	【手の動作】両鶏頭中段受け（両甲外向き）。	【手の動作】肘のスナップを使って両一本貫手中段落とし突き。
【足の動作】右足前猫足立ち。	【足の動作】立ち方はそのまま。	【足の動作】立ち方はそのまま。	【足の動作】寄り足で北へ飛び込む。
	【留意点】ゆっくり。		【留意点】気合い。

【Hands】
With both hands in Shuto, block Gedan-Kakiwake to either side of the body.

【Feet】
Nekoashidachi with right foot forward.

【Hands】
Keeping arms in on both sides, bring hands from low to high in a slightly curving motion from the inside.

【Feet】
Same as in ⑧②.

【Note】
Do slowly.

【Hands】
Chudan-Uke with both hands in 'Keito' (backs of the hands facing outward).

【Feet】
Same as in ⑧⑤.

【Hands】
Snapping both elbows, Ipponken Chudan Otoshiuke with both hands.

【Feet】
Jump towards north, using Yoriashi.

【Note】
Kiai.

挙動59〜61の解釈

◀相手の中段蹴りを手刀で掻き分け、さらに上段諸手突きを両鶏頭で受け、両一本貫手中段落とし突きで下腹部を攻撃する。

Block opponent's Chudangeri with Shuto-Gedan-Kakiwake, then block opponent's Jodan-Morotetsuki using Keito and attack Ippon-Nukite-Chudan-Otoshitsuki, using Ippon-Nukite with both hands, to the lower abomen.

挙動61	途中	挙動62	止め

後ろ

【手の動作】
両鶏頭中段受け。

【足の動作】
右足前猫足立ち。

【手の動作】
右掌（一本貫手）は前腕を立て、左掌の甲を右手の肘下にもっていく。

【足の動作】
左脚を軸に腰を左に回転し、右足を内側から弧を描きながらすり出し、南へ向く。

【留意点】
手足同時にゆっくり。

【手の動作】
右鶏頭中段受け。左掌右肘下。

【足の動作】
右足前猫足立ち。

【手の動作】
両拳を大腿部前にもっていく。

【足の動作】
左脚はそのままにして右足を引いてそろえ、八字立ち。

【Hands】
Chudan-Uke with both hands in 'Keito' (backs of the hands facing outward).

【Feet】
Nekoashidachi with right foot forward.

【Hands】
Point straight from forearm with Right-Ippon-Nukite, and bring the back of open left hand to under right elbow.

【Feet】
Using left leg as a pivot, twist hips to the left; slide out right foot by drawing an arc from inside to out, facing south.

【Note】
Both hands and feet move simultaneously and slowly.

【Hands】
Chudan-Uke with Right-Keito. Left hand is under right elbow.

【Feet】
Nekoashidachi with right foot forward.

【Hands】
Move both fists to in front of the thighs.

【Feet】
Keeping left foot in the same position pull in right foot so that both feet are aligned. Hachijidachi.

直立	礼	直立

【手の動作】
両手は開いて大腿部両側につけて伸ばす。

【足の動作】
左足、右足の順に閉じ、結び立ち。

※礼をする。

【手の動作】
手はそのまま。

【足の動作】
立ち方はそのまま。

【Hands】
Open both hands and stretch them along both thighs respectively.

【Feet】
Move the left foot, then the right foot, into Musubidachi.

※ Bow (Rei).

【Hands】
Same as in ❽.

【Feet】
Same as in ❽.

監修

（一財）全日本空手道松涛館　中央技術委員会

津山捷泰	Tsuyama Katsuhiro
澁谷　孝	Shibuya Takashi
西谷　賢	Nishitani Satoshi
阪梨　學	Sakanashi Manabu
香川政夫	Kagawa Masao
香川政義	Kagawa Masayoshi
山川和忠	Yamakawa Kazutada
永木　満	Nagaki Mitsuru

■編集協力

伊志嶺実	Ishimine Minoru
松江　肇	Matsue Hajime

■演武協力

在本幸司	Arimoto Koji
林田至史	Hayashida Chikashi

松涛館流空手道形教範全集　得意形Ⅰ　慈恩・観空大・抜塞大・五十四歩小・五十四歩大

2018年7月30日発行

編集	一般財団法人全日本空手道松涛館　中央技術委員会
編者	一般財団法人全日本空手道松涛館
発行	株式会社チャンプ
	〒166-0003　東京都杉並区高円寺南4-19-3 総和第二ビル
	電話：03-3315-3190（営業部）

©ALL Japan Karatedo Shotokan 2018
Printed in Japan　印刷：株式会社ナミ印刷

定価はカバーに表示してあります。
乱丁・落丁本は、ご面倒ですが(株)チャンプ宛にご送付ください。送料小社負担にてお取り替えいたします。

ISBN978-4-86344-021-0